Teachable Moments

A PARENT'S GUIDE TO HELPING YOUR CHILD EXCEL

Avor those teachable moments! Edie Weinthal

Edie Weinthal, Ph.D.
District Supervisor, English Education
The Pascack Valley Regional High School District
Montvale, New Jersey

BARRON'S

Dedication
To Gel, Bri, Sandi—as always. You are my dreams, my hopes, my possibilities.

Acknowledgments
Thank you to Wayne and Linda for all of the encouragement. Your support and your editorial advice have been invaluable. I am lucky to have had your guidance throughout this process.

All inquiries should be addressed to:
Barron's Educational Series, Inc.
250 Wireless Boulevard
Hauppauge, New York 11788
www.barronseduc.com

Library of Congress Control Number 2005043506

ISBN-13: 978-0-7641-3211-7
ISBN-10: 0-7641-3211-3

Library of Congress Cataloging-in-Publication Data

Weinthal, Edie.
Teachable moments : a parent's guide to helping your child excel / Edie Weinthal.
p. cm.
Includes bibliographical references (p.).
ISBN-13: 978-0-7641-3211-7
ISBN-10: 0-7641-3211-3
1. Education—Parent participation.   I. Title.

LB1048.5.W446 2006
371.1'92—dc22

2005043506

PRINTED IN THE UNITED STATES OF AMERICA

9 8 7 6 5 4 3 2 1

CONTENTS

INTRODUCTION

What exactly *is* a "super-student," and why would you want your child to become one? In the many years I have spent in education, I have taught students from kindergarten through college. Excellent students, at every level, exhibited the same type of traits: They were enthusiastic about learning, they had excellent organizational skills and study habits, they were passionate readers, and they were accomplished writers. These students, regardless of age or ability level, knew the thrill of working hard to achieve understanding; and they were happy because they perceived themselves as successful. It is never too late to start cultivating these qualities, and kindergarten is none too early to begin. Super-students come in all sizes, shapes, races, religions, and can be male or female. Some have short hair, some have long, some wear glasses, others do not. Some super-students may be athletes, while others prefer more sedentary hobbies. Every teacher knows a super-student when he or she sees one; even other students know the super-students in their classes. They are the students who are alert, prepared for school, genuinely curious about the curriculum, secure in their abilities, successful, and most often have the confidence that comes with a sense of high self-esteem. They are the students who are most often receiving higher grades and thereby obtaining access to many special advantages, including gifted and talented programs, special school awards and recognitions, honor roll status, and summer program opportunities. Later in their education, these same students continue to receive college scholarships and excellent job offers. As one considers the competition for seats in college classrooms and for jobs in this new century, it is apparent that students must maximize time spent in a classroom in order to enhance their critical thinking skills and to master lifelong learning techniques that can be transferable to any career choice.

One-third of your child's life will be spent in an educational setting. As so many parents know, the thousands of hours a child spends in a classroom may be a happy and rewarding experience or one filled with tears and frustration. Quite simply, a child who enjoys school, is confident about his or her abilities, and is excited and ready to learn will be much more ready to do so. A student does not need a super IQ to become a super-student. Learning to study and studying to learn are teachable skills, and parents can partner with teachers to make these components the fabric of a child's school experience. Students today are really smart; give them the how and the why and they will take that knowledge and soar.

It is imperative that you as parent collaborate with teachers to maximize your child's educational efforts. Some critics may feel that teaching *how to learn* should be solely the school's domain. Not in today's world. There are many reasons that teachers cannot work alone.

First, there is simply too much content information to be covered in the six hours per day a child spends in the classroom. Parents, however, have wonderful opportunities for "teachable moments" that can enhance any child's body of knowledge. For example, I recall one time when my son was about four years old and the whole family was out for a ride. He asked about writing a letter to his grandmother who lived in Florida. The conversation grew to an explanation of the entire U.S. postal system, and "the journey" of a letter from the time we put a stamp on the envelope until it reached Grandma's house.

Many classrooms today are quite full. Teachers have twenty, thirty, sometimes even more students in any one class. Although good teachers know how to modify their lessons to accommodate a wide variety of student learning styles, they cannot always give students individual explanations or the guided practices needed for every concept taught.

Another reason for involving yourself in your child's education is really quite simple: Your child wants to please *you*. Young children, as well as older students, respond positively to parental praise and pride. When students feel that you care about their performance, they will often double their efforts.

Many parents want to get involved in their child's schooling but feel they do not have the knowledge or expertise to do so. What teachers understand, however, is that a parent's influence on both a child's behavior and academic performance can help build the confidence and desire to continue achieving throughout life.

WHY THIS BOOK IS IMPORTANT FOR YOU— AND EVEN MORE SO FOR YOUR CHILD

Helping your child achieve success is neither quick nor easy. It is, rather, an ongoing process, one that takes conscientious effort over all the years that he or she is in school. However, the rewards for both you and your child are substantial. There are tangible rewards such as entry into prestigious summer programs, monetary scholarships to colleges, and opportunities for travel and study, as well as intangible rewards such as increased self-esteem, heightened confidence, and pride in oneself. Naturally, the earlier you begin reinforcing lifelong learning skills, the more time your child will have to internalize these skills and take ownership of his or her own learning.

Each chapter of this book delineates specific activities, actions, and attitudes that you can use to reinforce skills taught in school. Chapters are further divided chronologically so that you can readily access pertinent information depending upon your child's specific age and corresponding placement in school. Home involvement is imperative for building and reinforcing academic skills at *every* grade level and to maximize student learning and achievement. At home, "lessons" can become games, and students can learn without the pressures of constant assessment. This book is very much about seizing at-home learning opportunities and providing the message to children that education can be fun, challenging, exciting, and continuous throughout our lives. If students perceive of you as partners in their education, learning will simply be an extension of what you naturally do as a family. With your help and the tips in this book, your student will soon be on the path to realizing his or her full academic potential.

Chapter 1: Reading for Life

This chapter discusses the importance of reading from preschool through high school and provides hints for getting students to become "active" and enthusiastic readers.

Chapter 2: Writing to Learn

There is no skill more important than being able to express oneself in written form. This chapter discusses techniques parents can use to help students learn to write in an organized and concise fashion.

Chapter 3: Creating Excitement About School

This chapter discusses how to get students—from kindergarteners through high schoolers—excited about the upcoming school year. It also describes how to arrange a study space to optimize student concentration.

Chapter 4: Attending Back-to-School Night

It is important that parents go to back-to-school night, but it is equally important that they discuss the visit with their child. Learn what to "hear" from the teacher, and what to do with that information.

Chapter 5: Talking About Homework

The importance of parental involvement with homework cannot be overly emphasized. This chapter explains the appropriate degree of parental involvement and advises when parents should allow students time to be independent.

Chapter 6: Reading the Newspaper

Fact: Students do not read enough nonfiction. This chapter explains how reading the newspaper daily can enhance student knowledge, reading, and vocabulary ability, and how these few minutes each day can prepare students for achievement on high-stakes tests.

Chapter 7: Researching for Answers

Believe it or not, students in kindergarten are now attempting to produce basic "research" papers! This chapter discusses how parents can serve as resource partners to help students learn one of the most important skills for the new century.

Chapter 8: Using the Computer

It is taken for granted that this generation of students will need to be conversant with multimedia technology. Parents and students may even reverse roles as they work together to access the vast array of knowledge now available via the computer.

CHAPTER

1

READING FOR LIFE

*. . . If I were a young person today, trying to gain a sense of
myself in the world, I would do that again by reading,
just as I did when I was young.*
—Maya Angelou

Today, more than ever, your child will need to have substantial
reading and writing skills to compete favorably in school, college, and in the job market. Our "information age" demands that we
read, sort, and critically analyze massive amounts of written and
visual information at a rate that could not possibly have been
predicted even fifty years ago. Reading skills are essential in every
subject taught in school. Quite simply, the earlier children become
proficient in reading and writing, the better the chances for academic success.

One of the most important things that you, as a parent, can do
for your young child, is to give him or her foundation skills in reading. Children need to develop a love for reading from a very early
age, and it is up to parents to foster this love. Students who start
school with a love of books are usually excited to learn new reading
skills.

Older students who are "proficient" readers will discover
numerous advantages to reading well and reading often: Homework
takes less time, schoolwork is easier to comprehend, and books can
be endless sources of knowledge and entertainment.

Preschool, Kindergarten, and Younger Elementary School Learners

PREPARING YOUR CHILD FOR SUCCESS

Volumes have been written on the importance of talking and reading to your child at a very early age. In truth, the seeds for early reading can never be planted too early. Here are some tips on how you can prepare your preschooler for success by encouraging an early love of reading.

Buy your child books.

A teacher reports that at her house, birthdays, Christmas, and all special occasions were always celebrated with purchases of books. Her children learned to value books, and to this day her (now-adult) children still love to receive books from her. Surround your own children with books and they will grow up feeling that books are a natural part of a person's "landscape."

Read to your child.

There is no age limit to reading to your child—infants through high school students love having stories read to them. Sitting in a rocking chair and reading to a very young child can became your "quiet time" together, a few minutes of peace, sanity, and bonding in an otherwise chaotic day. As the child grows older, the reading sessions can also grow longer and longer; parents can progress from looking at picture books, to the telling of simple stories, to reading lengthy adventure tales. Make this commitment to read daily and it will become something your child learns to value. It works well to *schedule* reading in the same place, at about the same time each day. Don't let anything or anyone interfere with your reading time. Very soon it will become a routine that your child considers a treat: time alone with you and a chance to exercise his or her imagination. It doesn't get better than that!

Model reading for your child.

When children see that reading is valued in a household, they most often become readers themselves. Children need to see that mothers, fathers, and older siblings find reading enjoyable and relaxing. At an early age they will want to emulate what they see. If Dad is reading in a big, comfortable, overstuffed chair, a toddler will often want to bring his or her book to that very chair and "read like Daddy." As children get older, talk to them about the books you are reading. Children need to know that books can open up entire new worlds to them: worlds of ideas, thoughts, stories, and information. They learn this by hearing you speak about the books you are reading.

Get your child a library card.

Almost all public libraries now have "story hour" for preschoolers and many other community events for older children. With their very own library card, children feel connected to a community of readers, and they see for themselves the vast array of books that will be available to them once they, too, become avid readers. Libraries are open in the evenings and on the weekends, so if you work you can still make weekly trips to the library a part of your child's regular routine.

Promote oral language skills, word games, and communication skills.

Reading actually begins as an auditory skill. Parents can build a reading foundation by talking, reading, and playing rhyming games with their children. As a child's vocabulary grows, he or she begins to recognize more and more words, thus helping with decoding when an attempt at actual reading eventually occurs. A large vocabulary will help a child read and comprehend new material in elementary and high school, since all new knowledge is built upon prior knowledge. For example, if you have discussed *migration* with your child, he or she will have little difficulty recognizing the word when encountering it in written form for the first time.

Adopt a positive attitude.

When you work with your child, at any level of reading instruction, you must remain in a positive, enthusiastic frame of mind. Reading is all about readiness; if your child isn't ready, do not force the issue—there is no sense in making any session overly stressful. The most important thing you can do is praise his or her accomplishments, however small, and keep the reading session fun for both of you. If you are negative or too demanding, your child will begin to consider reading a burden or chore. Never, *ever* punish a child who doesn't want to read—just put the book away and try again in a few days or weeks.

Learning Games and Activities

In addition to instilling a love of reading in your preschooler, you may also want to enhance his or her pre-reading skill development by playing any number of fun and educational learning activities together. Children are eager to learn when letters and words connect to the realities of their own daily lives. The following ideas will start preschool parents thinking in the right direction.

Alphabet Games

The "Alphabet Song" is probably more recognized than "America the Beautiful," by adults as well as children. After all, it is the way most of us learned our alphabet. (Admit it. Some of us *still* occasionally sing the song when we have to file alphabetically!) In addition to singing the ABC song, there are a myriad of alphabet activities to do with your younger child. The goal is for your child to recognize the shapes of the letters and eventually link them with their appropriate sounds. Start, for example, with his or her name. Children love to see a sign and identify it with their own name. They can point to it proudly and tell visitors "that's me!"

Don't forget those inexpensive alphabet magnets for your refrigerator. Let your child manipulate those letters to form his or her name or other words.

Letter-of-the-Week

Celebrate a different letter each week! Serve alphabet cereal and see how many *A*s or *B*s or *C*s your child can find. Make a letter-of-the-week book by stapling together several sheets of paper with the letter of the week printed boldly at the top of each sheet. Your child can "illustrate" the pages with things that start with that letter. Children can use stickers, pictures from magazines or newspapers, or even computer clip art to illustrate things that begin with each letter. Crayons or markers can be used by children who want to draw pictures for themselves. He or she can later "read" the book to you. Alphabet cookies or pancakes in the shape of the weekly letter make both eating and pre-reading fun for your child. Remember that having the same letter for an entire week will reinforce the shape and sound of each letter as alphabet learning becomes a fun game.

Sight-Word Games

Car time presents a wonderful opportunity to reinforce many pre-reading skills while making driving a lot more pleasant.

"Find something that begins with the letter *A* . . ." is a game children love to play. Another fun car activity is letter identification. "Who can find the T in Target?" "Who can find the X in Texaco?" Car games such as these jump-start whole-language instruction as youngsters learn to "read" signs, logos, and advertising billboards.

Food Fun

The kitchen is another wonderful source for introducing pre-reading skills. Dough, for example, is an ideal medium for shaping letters and can occupy young children for a great length of time. This activity not only builds reading readiness, but also teaches children to focus on tasks for extended periods of time, a skill that will serve them well in later school years. As youngsters help you prepare meals and snacks in the kitchen, they can also practice counting skills, measuring skills, and shape recognition, all while building a richer working vocabulary.

Although this section is about reading, it should be noted that kitchen play can also be an endless source for developing solid math concepts that will serve children well in later years. Measurement concepts and mathematical vocabulary can all be practiced in the casual and "fun" environment of the kitchen. As you have children fill containers with water or other substances, discuss what they are doing by using words like *more, less, empty, full, greater than* or *less than, how much, how many, count, subtract, add,* and *enough.* These terms all encourage mathematical thinking and build important vocabulary skills.

The supermarket can also be an endless source of new reading experiences for the young child. They will point to familiar packages of their favorite foods long before they can read the names on the cans or boxes. They will recognize "goodies" and spot them on the shelves. Encourage this recognition and point to the letters on the product as you put it in your cart.

The Singing–Reading Connection

Oral language predated the written word, and one cannot underestimate the powerful connection between hearing, speaking, and eventually reading. Singing and chanting games that parents play with children actually help lay the foundation for later reading skills. Those early poems and rhymes engage children in hearing and repeating word patterns, memorizing vocabulary, and learning language construction. After singing "Three Blind Mice," for several years, children who are ready will initially "read" the words from memory when they first encounter them in written form. This pretend reading has several important functions. Children will have made the connection from the oral to the printed word, and they will have a great deal of confidence about their initial reading skills. Remember, children love to read the words of songs they already know. After a few readings, ask your child to find certain letters. Ask them, for example, to find the "M" for mice, or the "B" for blind. This initial reading lesson can expand until students learn the sounds for an entire word and eventually will recognize that word outside of the context of the song. Make an early investment in a traditional book of nursery rhymes and make the rhymes a part of your nightly reading routine. Children will eventually identify their favorite poems and ask for them again and again. As you read, point to the key words and make connections with the pictures that are always found in this type of book.

Using songs that translate into reading experiences is not useful exclusively with preschool children. One inner-city reading instructor used rap music to encourage reading among middle school students. The students were not proficient readers, but they knew and enjoyed favorite rap artists. The teacher successfully used the words of the rap music to encourage students to practice their reading skills with familiar words.

Picture-Matching Games

Preschool children love matching games. You can buy them in any bookstore, find them on the Internet, or create them yourself with old magazines. "Find the picture that starts with . . ." reinforces the alphabet and helps students remember initial letter sounds. Another game you can play with your youngster is a variation of the traditional game, "Concentration." Create a set of playing cards using some or all of the letters of the alphabet. (Make two cards for each letter.) Place the cards face down on a table and have the child turn over two cards. If two letters match, the child keeps the cards. If a match is not found, the cards are turned back over until the next turn. The player with the most pairs at the end of the game wins.

What's in the Bag?

This activity is a wonderful opportunity for enhancing creativity and original thinking. It also promotes storytelling, organizational, and critical-thinking skills. "What's in the Bag?" is an invitation for toddlers to play with vocabulary as they manipulate items that are both familiar and unfamiliar. Fill a plain paper bag with an assortment of items. You might put in the bag a crayon, a small stuffed animal, a flower, an apple, and a magnet. Have your child try to tell a story using the items in the bag as story props. Here's one possible story:

*One day, Johnny felt very sad. He wanted to go out to play but it was raining. He sat in his room, by the window, holding his **stuffed animal** named Fluffy. All of a sudden he got an idea! He ran to his desk and got a **crayon**. He began to draw a picture of a pretty*

flower. *The flower picture made him happy. He brought the picture to show his mother. She loved the picture and used a new* **magnet** *to hang his picture in the kitchen. Johnny was happy when he and his mother sat down at the kitchen table to share a bright, red* **apple** *for a snack.*

In another variation of this game, the child simply pulls out the items one by one and identifies the "beginning letter" of each one.

One final note: The Internet is a vast source for games and reading readiness activities for younger children. There are sites that have manipulatives for storytelling activities, sites that allow children to illustrate stories that they have invented, and sites that give parents and teachers all sorts of pre-reading projects to do with younger children. There are thousands upon thousands of short stories for children that can be downloaded from various Web sites. In fact, many fine children's books are just a mouse-click away! Children begin computer skills as early as kindergarten; if you have access to technology at home, you might consider taking advantage of this incredible resource as a tool for reading readiness activities.

Elementary and Middle School Readers

Let's jump ahead a few years. Your child is now in elementary school and is possibly a fairly proficient reader, reading at or above grade level. However, your job is far from finished. Remediation, skill maintenance, and/or enrichment for more advanced students, rely upon ongoing reinforcement at home in order to improve a child's academic standing and raise grades and test scores.

Students still need to see reading modeled at home. Hopefully, earlier training has prevailed, and students have learned to fall asleep with a good book rather than to the noise of a blasting television. As children get older, parents can pass along favorite books they read while they were growing up—books that have become classics in youth and young adult literature. Think back to the favorite stories and authors of your childhood. If your memory needs refreshing, just spend a few minutes in the children's section of your local library. You may be surprised by the number of titles you remember! If, by chance, you were never a reader, ask the children's librarian for suggested titles. There are a wide variety of literary awards given to young adult literature, and these can also guide your selection.

Remember, as students get older, it is important that you discuss what you are reading, too. So many students are motivated to become "readers" because they are excited about reading a particular book, even if that book might be far above their current reading level. Interest level goes a long way toward whetting a child's appetite for reading, despite the difficulty of the reading task.

REINFORCING READING SKILLS AT HOME

The following are some at-home activities that can help reinforce elementary and middle school reading proficiencies and that will build academic skills for high school and beyond.

Following Directions

Reading and following directions figure prominently in all test-taking situations, yet are rarely practiced outside of a school setting. There are quite a few ways that you can reinforce these skills:

- **Reading map directions** teaches students sequential thinking skills and orderly and logical progression of ideas. On road trips, invite your child be the "navigator" and have him or her read directions as you drive to new places.

- For fun, have your child **write out driving directions** to a familiar place. Then, actually drive to that place following the *exact* directions as he or she wrote them. Your child will learn the importance of clear specific, step-by-step instructions the first time they omit an important turn.

■ Another variation of this activity is for your child to **write out specific directions for a simple task**. The task can be as simple as making a peanut butter and jelly sandwich, tying one's shoes, or even getting on a bicycle. Once your child writes out the instructions, you try to follow the directions exactly. (Watch out—if it doesn't say "pick up a knife" to spread the peanut butter, then you might have to do it with your fingers!) The results of this little game can be very amusing, but at the same time they reinforce important reading and writing skills. This exercise can be done with kindergarten as well as high school students, and both groups will equally enjoy the challenge.

Finding Facts

Reading is all about finding facts. It is a skill that students need when they study, and it is a skill that most reading components of high-stakes tests attempt to assess. Teaching students to read for facts can be a treasure hunt game that enhances both reading and research skills. Here are a few ideas for practicing "fact-finding" at home:

■ Comb the newspaper together with your child and **locate two ads** for a similar product (for example, two ads for ice cream). Invite your child to examine both ads to identify and compare various things about the products. More advanced youngsters can be challenged to figure out the cost differential between the two items and exercise a bit of math expertise at the same time.

■ Encourage **reading an article** from the daily newspaper. If the article is difficult, read it with your child. After the article is read, use the "four W's" to discuss the article: Who was this about? What happened? When did it happen? Where did this happen? See more about this in Chapter 6: Reading the Newspaper.

■ Let your child help you **look up information in the telephone directory**. In addition to practicing alphabetizing skills by finding actual phone numbers, students can use the front of the telephone guide to find out all sorts of interesting information. Play games to locate zip codes in a different state, to find places to purchase unusual items, to look up people with different professions, or to find entertainment venues.

■ Older students can learn to use keyword searches to perform **research on the Internet**, a place that opens up a virtually unlimited store of information waiting to be discovered. Make it a game by posing a nightly challenge question and see how quickly your child can uncover an answer. Here are a few questions just to give you some ideas. Naturally, the questions can be adapted for differing ability and age levels.

❏ Where can we board the cat/dog if we go on vacation?

❏ Where can a person go horseback riding in New York City?

❏ What is a peccary and where does it live?

❏ Where would you have the greatest chance to see a moose in the wild?

❏ Are there any doll hospitals in the United States?

❏ How might I learn about the value of a rare stamp?

❏ What do I need to plan for a trip to Australia?

❏ How many female race car drivers win major races every year?

You can have fun making up these types of questions, depending on your own child's interests and maturity.

Building Vocabulary

Naturally, the single most effective way to build vocabulary is to keep reading extensively. But there are all kinds of vocabulary games—from Scrabble and Mad Libs to crossword puzzles and acrostics—that also enhance vocabulary instruction. In addition, as you read to or with your child, ask him or her for other words that have the same or different meanings as key words in the text. For example, if you come upon the word *amazing*, talk about all of the other words that have similar meanings (*remarkable, surprising, wonderful*). Word games that play with synonyms (words that are the same) and antonyms (words that have opposite meanings) are also tremendous vocabulary builders.

Resist the urge to tell children the meaning of new words. Be patient and allow them time to read a word they may find difficult. If they encounter an unknown word in a reading selection, first show them how to "guess" using context clues. In a given sentence, what might this word mean? What is another word that might make sense in this sentence? Show students how to "break down" new words by identifying prefixes or suffixes that can help determine meaning. If a child doesn't know the word *mistrust*, perhaps they know *trust*. Teach them the prefix *mis* and then discover how many other words also have this same beginning. Show them how *ist* can be added to the end of a word to signify a person who does something (*artist, cartoonist, physicist*). Prefix and suffix practice can be rapid vocabulary building tools. Reading and learning the meaning of new words will help build self-esteem when children are praised for mastering a new word independently.

Keeping a Journal

Middle school children love to keep journals and diaries. Encourage your child to "free write" in a special notebook or diary after a reading session. Free writes are simply personal reactions to a reading. This type of writing is sometimes called a "reaction journal" because it serves as a way for students to record initial, emotional reactions to something they have read.

Finding High Interest Books

It is so important, particularly in the middle school years, for children to continue to be avid readers. However, these become the years that so many other interests invade a child's life—and it is often difficult for parents to battle the lure of sports, friends, Play Station, or trips to the mall. Parents need to discover ways to use those other interests to keep students reading.

One important way to do this is to find books about your child's interests. There are so many books written about every conceivable subject, that it is almost impossible not to find *something* that can interest every child. There are books on dinosaurs, ball players, ballet dancers, animals, policemen, cars, skiing, stamps, computers, baking, and millions of other topics of interest. Use the Internet to search for appropriate titles by typing in the key word to any search engine.

A colleague recently told me that she and her family have family book nights. Instead of going to a movie, the entire family goes over to a book shop close to her house. There, each member of the family gets to select a new book; they then find a comfortable spot to begin reading as they wait for one another. The larger bookshops even have small café areas where one can sip a drink, have a snack, and get lost in a good book.

High School:
Becoming Active Readers

High school is a time to build on prior skills and to perfect academic patterns of behavior that will serve students well in higher educational settings. Unless a child is in a remedial English class, there will be very few lessons on reading *strategies* at this stage of his or her education. Students at this stage are expected to employ a wide range of previously learned strategies in order to interact with words and to create meaning from a wide variety of texts.

Previously formed habits such as scheduling reading sessions and managing time, effective study habits, reading critically, taking notes from a textbook, effective marking and underlining, and speed and comprehension skills will all come into play by the time your student is in high school.

WHAT YOUR TEEN IS READING

Before discussing some of the techniques that students can use to become more effective readers and, consequently, better students, it is important to note that there is a vast array of different *types* of reading materials available to this age group. This is important to note because many different reading strategies come into play depending upon the subject and type of material one chooses.

First, students will be reading nonfiction. Nonfiction includes their various textbooks, whether science, math, social studies, or other subjects. It also may include biographies and autobiographies, essays, selections from journals and magazines, newspapers, and even articles from the Internet. Some students may enjoy reading factual books on topics that interest them—from dinosaurs or space exploration to cooking or fine arts. At the very least, students should be encouraged to read a daily newspaper or to subscribe to an online news service. This daily reading is the best practice for learning to read well and for learning important strategies for critical reading. (Chapter 6 discusses more extensively daily and weekly use of the newspaper.)

Fiction is another genre that students should be reading both in and outside of school. The high school curriculum often focuses on fictional works from various time periods, from different countries, and from multiple cultural perspectives. Throughout high school, students read novels, plays, and short stories that may be fictional. There are countless lists of books for high school students published on the Internet; these are books with which well-read students should probably be familiar by the end of their high school career. You should try to read some of the titles along with your teenager; familial discussion makes the reading of any book much more enriching for the student. The *New York Times* Best Seller List should not be overlooked as a reading resource for the high school student. As a starting point for your high schooler, refer to the recommended titles listed at the back of this book.

At this age, students often discover a favorite contemporary author and begin reading multiple books by the same writer. Some of these authors, like Dean Koontz, write science fiction. Other young adults enjoy the romantic novels of authors such as Danielle Steele or Belva Plain, or mysteries by Mary Higgins Clark. What is important here is not the content of the novel, but the fact that students are continually reading and are learning the power of a book to teach, to soothe, or to transport a person to a different time, place, or mood. That regular trip to the library that was started when the child was in preschool should, at this stage, be a normal part of the student's life.

Trips to the library can be augmented by trips to bookstores in order to keep students continually supplied with books of interest. Choice is an important component to continuous reading. Let's face it. High school students have a tremendous amount of demands placed upon their time. Studies, sports, outside interests, religious activities, social engagements, jobs, and family commitments all compete for reading time. If your student can only manage to read for a few minutes before bed, he or she should spend that short time relaxing with a favorite author. During weekends and on vacation time, reading for *pleasure* should be encouraged so that reading becomes as essential to his or her well-being as eating properly or getting enough exercise.

CLASSROOM CLOSEUP

Brian and Samantha are both eleventh-grade students with similar IQs and no learning disabilities. Brian is an avid reader and often has more than one book started at a time. Because he uses an array of reading strategies depending upon what he is reading, he usually completes his nightly homework in a reasonable period of time. He often has time available to review or recopy his classroom notes, to read supplementary materials, or to pursue reading for his own pleasure. Brian has a large vocabulary and can often understand new words using context clues. He has been a "reader" since his early years, and he is comfortable with oral reading, silent reading, skimming new materials, and thinking critically about a given text. He is excited when his teachers begin new books, and he is enthusiastic and self-confident about encountering new information. Brian has scored well on the verbal portion of the high school standardized test, and looks forward to proving himself on the college admission test.

Samantha is a more reticent reader. For her, reading is a laborious process which she does unwillingly. Samantha reads every word and often has to reread sentences in order to understand their meaning. She finds that after five or ten minutes her concentration wanes, and she simply stares unseeingly at the words. Samantha's nightly homework takes far too long and she often must go to bed with some of it unfinished. She reads everything the "same" way, and does not always understand the purpose for the reading. Samantha has few, if any, strategies for "attacking" a text, and needs extra time to process information. Samantha never reads for pleasure, for reading is not pleasurable. She dreads the teacher introducing a new book, and will never make eye contact with the teacher unless she is called on to read aloud. Samantha is taking a prep course for the college admissions test, but has no confidence that she will do well enough to attend the college of her choice.

Brian and Samantha are not exaggerated cases but rather real students. Certainly, some students have natural talents and abilities, but much of what made Brian a "super-student" can be taught to others. Excellent students may be born, but they can also be made! Let's examine some of the essential qualities of excellent readers and focus on ways that you can support your student as he or she moves toward super-student status by becoming a powerful reader and thinker.

The first thing you need to do is simply observe your child as he or she reads. Try to be discreet and casually take note of his or her reading habits. Jot down all the things that you observe.

- Where does he or she read? (At a desk? In bed? In a comfortable chair?)

- Does he or she read with a finger under each and every word?

- Do the lips move when he or she reads?

- Does your child lose focus and often glance up from the material or gaze out the window?

- Does he or she stop every few words to look up new vocabulary in a dictionary?

- When your child is given a specific reading assignment, what does he or she do first? (Does he or she "Preview" the assignment, get paper and pencil, or just "jump" into the reading?)

Use the answers to the above questions as a starting point for helping to improve your teen's critical reading skills. The problems and solutions are discussed next.

READING: HOW IMPORTANT IS SPEED?

Reading is to the mind what exercise is to the body.
—Richard Steele, 1672–1729

As previously stated, frequent reading is the best way to learn to read well. It is also the single most important factor toward building reading speed. Just like exercise, the more one reads, the easier it becomes. Good readers learn "shortcuts" to help them through the reading process. It is important, also, to realize that every genre requires a different reading rate. An adventure novel can surely be read much more quickly than a physics textbook. Students need to learn how to speed up and how to slow down, depending upon the material being read. Reading speed may often have to be adjusted based on how difficult or easy it is for the student to comprehend the reading.

As our eyes move across a given page of print, we take in the words that are on each page. In order to increase reading speed, it is necessary to take in more words at each glance. Good readers don't make their eyes move faster but see groups of words rather than one word at a time. For example, the above sentence might look like this to a slow reader: *Good/readers/don't/make/their/eyes/move/faster/but/see/groups/of/words/rather/than/one/word/at/a/time.* A rapid reader would read the sentence in this manner: *Good readers/don't make their eyes move faster/but see groups of words/rather than one word at a time.*

Like any other skill, reading gets better with practice. There are many exercises that your child can do to build up reading speed and comprehension, thus becoming a stronger and more proficient reader.

Make Speed Reading a Game.

Your child can practice reading groups of words by playing timed games. Find a long passage from a newspaper or magazine, and pick out a specific phrase buried in the passage. See how fast your child can find the group of words. Practice this game until his or her speed increases significantly. The passages can get longer and longer, as the reader becomes more and more proficient with this exercise.

Learn to Skim for Important Information.

One way to increase reading speed is to practice skimming. When skimming, the eyes are forced to move more rapidly than usual down the page. Some skimming methods recommend the use of a hand or an index card to force the eyes down a page of text. Skimming should happen at a much faster rate than normal reading. Encourage your child to spend a few minutes each day skimming various materials. You will probably find that after practicing skimming, his or her normal reading rate will dramatically increase.

There Is a Purpose for Everything One Reads.

It is important that your child understand the "purpose" for which he or she is reading. For example, when looking for a specific piece of information, it is not necessary to read every word in a text. For more details on reading for a purpose, see the information below on "SQ3R."

Reading Adds Up.

Quantity counts! Encourage your child to read more each day. According to one source, just fifteen minutes a day of reading an average size novel equals eighteen books a year at an average reading speed.

Practice Makes Reading Easier.

If a child is having difficulty sustaining long periods of reading, practice shorter reading periods daily. Start with five to ten minutes of sustained reading and gradually increase the time. Just like an athlete who practices by building up endurance, reading concentration can improve with practice.

READING TO COMPREHEND, READING TO LEARN

If you were to observe effective readers, whether they are reading a novel or a work of nonfiction, you would notice that they usually start a new reading in the same way. They "handle" the book, looking at the cover, the back of the book, the table of contents, the date of publication, the preface, the dedications or foreword notes, the diagrams and pictures, if any, and they flip through the pages, looking at the general organization of the text. What they are actually doing is "pre-reading," and it is an important step that can save hours of time and maximize each reading session.

One valuable system of pre-reading and then reading effectively is called the SQ3R Reading Method. The acronym SQ3R stands for "Survey, Question, Read, Recite, Review." This method has been found to be a successful reading and study skill tool for countless readers. Some people add a "P" in front of the SQ3R, which stands for "purpose."

1. Purpose

The student needs to ask, "Why am I reading this selection?" If it is to answer a specific question (for example, "What did the Lewis & Clark expedition accomplish?"), then he or she can stop reading when that question is answered. Finding a specific answer may call for a simple method of *skimming* the text until the required information is found. If a student is looking for a main idea, a specific fact, evidence, an example, or a relationship, a minimal amount of time can be spent in the actual reading of the material.

2. Survey

Often, a teacher will assign a complete chapter or more to be read by the student. Stop! The next five minutes may be the most important step of the entire assignment. The student should not jump directly into reading before completing this crucial step. A reader should always "survey" the chapter before actually starting to read. How does one properly survey a chapter?

- First, look at the title, the bold-faced headings, and the subheadings. The title should explain the main theme of the chapter. "Westward Expansion" or "Crocodiles and Alligators" tell specifically what a chapter is (and is *not*) about. A reader can now anticipate the type of information to be found in a given reading and is prepared for what is ahead.

- Next, survey the charts, maps, or pictures that may be in the chapter. If there is a map showing the route of westward expansion or a chart comparing crocodiles and alligators, the visual information is also helpful in preparation for reading.

■ Skim the introductory and concluding paragraphs. Frequently, these contain much of the chapter information in a concise form, and the actual reading will later help put these into context.

■ Note if there is a "summary" at the end of the chapter. Summaries usually highlight the important points of each chapter and give the reader a mental outline to follow while reading.

3. Question

The next step in the SQ3R method is a very simple task that can be learned in a few practice sessions. The student looks at the titles, headings, and subheadings and turns them into questions. So, for example, "Social Consequences of Industrialization" becomes "What were the social consequences of industrialization?" "The Origin of Vertebrates" becomes "What was the origin of vertebrates?" Other questions might begin with *who, where, how,* or *why.* Students should write these questions into a notebook so they can be used as headings for note taking during the reading. The questions should be listed on the left-hand side of the paper, leaving the right column free for answers. (See the following page.) During the "recite" portion of the SQ3R method, the right-hand side will be covered so the student can perform a self-test on the material read. This step ensures that the student is reading for specific answers to pertinent questions—and that in itself focuses the reading and prepares the brain for the information the reading should yield.

Who was Konstantin Pobedonostsev?	• A dominant figure in the court of Alexander III. • Distrusted western ideas concerning freedom of thought, civil liberties, and constitutions.
What was his relationship to Alexander III?	• He was his former tutor.
How did he influence Russian policies?	• used religion to restore spiritual communion between the Russian people and the Tsar. • Secret police given new power. • Begins persecution against revolutionaries; increase in censorship, passports regulating travel, government supervision of education.

Some students also find it helpful to complete a "knowledge chart" before the initial reading. After turning the headings into questions, students briefly list the "answers" or things they already know about the topic. After reading the text, students fill in a second column with the new facts they learned. A knowledge chart might start out looking like this:

Prior knowledge about The Beatles	New knowledge about The Beatles
1. From England	1.
2. Long hair	2.
3. Paul McCartney, John Lennon, George Harrison, Ringo Starr	3.

4. Read

As the student begins the actual reading, he or she should read to find answers to the questions created in the previous step. Reading speed should vary. If a section does not seem to contain the answer to one of the questions, that section can be read at a more rapid pace. The reader should slow down, however, for difficult passages and for passages that appear to hold the answers to questions. Highlighting the sentences that contain the required answers is the optimum approach, but, realistically, most textbooks must be returned to the teacher unmarked at the end of each school year. An acceptable alternative is to use "post-it" notes to mark pages and passages that hold important information. The reader can return to these later and record the needed information.

Students working in this manner become *active* readers. They do not passively read; rather, they interact with the text itself. They ask questions, prioritize materials, and accept or reject textual information based on need. Students use high-level critical-thinking skills as they concentrate on finding answers to a predicted informational framework.

As students read through a chapter, they should also make certain to reread the graphs, pictures, headings, and charts to check their applicability to the questions.

When your reader initially practices this new method of power reading, have him or her read only one chapter section at a time. After reading each section, the student should proceed to the "Recite" step below.

5. Recite

This is the step that feels the most awkward to many students. Reciting feels too much like "talking to yourself," an action that they have come to associate with strange behavior. However, research has shown that learning can be strengthened by adding more senses to the experience. Seeing (or reading) the text, coupled with saying and/or hearing the material, makes the content of the reading much easier to remember. The writing component further "cements" the material so that students can easily reflect and refer to their notes after reading.

After reading the first section of a chapter, a student should attempt to summarize what he or she has just read. Ideally, students should try to orally answer the initial questions from their reading. If they are uncomfortable answering aloud, they should instead write out the answers to the questions using their own words and information from the text. If they do both steps, so much the better. Eventually, the recite step becomes second nature as students move more rapidly through the SQ3R process. Each section of the chapter should be read with notes taken in this manner.

6. Review

Review is an ongoing process that begins at the initial contact with a text and takes students up to the time the material will actually be tested. It has been found that brief reviews over several days are much more effective for authentic learning than the typical "cram" session that often occurs the night before a test or quiz.

After writing the answers to the questions on the right-hand side of the page, students should review them one final time before finishing the reading session. Just a glance over these notes should solidify the information that was read and ensure that all important points in the chapter were noted. Once a student has written good notes, the text need not be reread; it serves merely as a resource for clarification if needed.

The day following the initial reading, students should fold over the right side of the paper, leaving the questions exposed. Students can then attempt, either in writing or orally, to answer the questions to the best of their ability. Once the page is unfolded to check answers, students should make note of those questions with which they had difficulty. Perhaps they might even choose to create additional study aids for these particular facts.

A night or two before a test, parents can help by reviewing the material with the student. Have your child explain the answers in his or her own words, while you use the notes on the right side of the page to check for accuracy. When your student "teaches" you the material in this way, it represents the highest level of learning and understanding. If he or she can make the topic understandable to you, it is likely that they will do well on any test the teacher may create.

BECOMING A CRITICAL READER

You can help your child become a more critical reader as you discuss a given text with him or her. As students read more and more, they need to become aware of specific techniques used by writers to influence readers. In other words, they should move to become discerning and critical readers, questioning not only the topics themselves, but the purpose and context of every text they read. As students read, they must think about the issues being discussed and the conclusions a given author reaches about those issues. Some possible topics for discussion would be:

What issues is the author addressing?

What are the author's feelings about the issues?

How does the author defend (or refute) his or her position?

What are the author's reasons for his or her position?

Does the author use facts, opinions, theories, or examples to support the position?

What does an examination of the author's language show? (Are the words positive/negative/emotional/neutral?)

How does what the author has written connect with "reality" as you know it?

Students who think critically about a given text are interacting on a very high level with that reading. As students think critically, they also learn to think independently and creatively. This "practice" discussion with you gives the student's ideas time to "percolate"; the next day in class he or she will have many more insights and a much more productive discussion than will those classmates who were not given the opportunity to discuss the reading in advance. Once again, pre-thinking yields a greater self-confidence, and self-confidence translates into better performance—and, ultimately, into better grades.

CHAPTER

2

WRITING TO LEARN, LEARNING TO WRITE

How do I know what I think until I see what I say?
—E.M. Forster

There are many purposes for writing. We write for pleasure, for practical reasons, for job-related reasons, for therapeutic reasons, and for social reasons. We write to express simple ideas, to express something we have learned, to convince an audience of our point of view, to convey very specific information, or to challenge another's opinion or interpretation.

Writing is essential to learning. It is a critical skill to master if one is to become an excellent student. Writing is a tool students will use from kindergarten through college, and helping your child learn to communicate through writing provides a skill that is practical, stimulating, self-expressive, and lifelong. As the above quote indicates, writing is an act that is intricately tied to thinking. Writing clarifies thinking and assists students in communicating their ideas to others. Learning to write well requires patience, practice, clear thinking, a meaningful task, encouragement, and an interested audience. Active learners, precise thinkers, and good communicators are not born but made, and this chapter will give parents some key information on how to encourage children to write to learn.

Preschool, Kindergarten, and Younger Elementary School Learners

In English, we use the term "writing" to indicate the skill of forming letters—as well as to indicate the skill of constructing and explaining ideas by putting those ideas on paper. These are not the same skills at all. The printing of letters is a mechanical skill and children will learn those through practice. In fact, many of the ideas in the previous chapter, "Reading for Life," will help encourage preschoolers to learn to form the letters of the alphabet. This chapter, however, will explore the other meaning of "writing"—writing to understand and to put forth ideas, often known as "writing to learn."

One of the first means of written communication for children is through drawing. Preschool children should be encouraged to talk about their artwork and to tell stories about it. Ask your child questions: Who is this girl/boy? What is this person doing? Can you tell me a story about this picture? Some children may even try to write their own stories. Don't worry if the letters aren't correct or if words are not spelled out correctly. Instead, show an interest in the story, ask questions about it, encourage your child to talk about the story, and be enthusiastic whenever he or she tries to write. Children experiment with pretend writing before they actually write in school. They scribble, they draw, they write their names, they invent stories and characters, and they play at "writing" books.

Young children have stories they want to share long before they learn all of the formal rules for writing, speaking, and correct grammatical usage. Luckily, you do not need to wait until children are proficient at writing before encouraging their endeavors. There are many fun activities to do with early writers that will help spark their interest in writing. Most important, your child needs to hear your response to his or her writing; in the initial phases of writing do not focus on the errors, for there will be many, but rather comment on the thoughts, descriptions, and creative ideas in your child's writing. The following are some initial writing activities to do with young children.

Reading and Writing Connection

If your child reads good books, he or she will become a better writer. Use your child's favorite bedtime story. Consider asking your child to imagine what happened *before* the beginning of the story took place, or what happened *after* the actual story ended. Your child can make up his or her own story based on their favorite characters, and you can write a new "book" for your child. Do not be concerned if these initial stories are plagiarized. Children will gradually move to more original accounts as they practice story telling and writing. What is important here is the use of their imagination and their excitement at putting together a story of their own.

Writing a "Report"

Believe it or not, preschoolers can learn to write elementary reports with information they learn. For example, many young children are fascinated by dinosaurs. How about a dinosaur report? Have your child dictate to you all the dinosaurs he or she may know. Next, ask what they might like to tell people about dinosaurs. (For example, your "writer" might wish to describe what dinosaurs ate, where they slept, or how big they were.) The idea here is to show your child that words can help categorize and organize information. After you make a list of facts, put the words into sentences. (Tyrannosaurus Rex was a gigantic dinosaur. He lived a long time ago. He ate meat.) If you have access to a computer, your child might want to import some pictures into the report. Let the child illustrate the report, decorate a title page or cover, and bind it together as a book. By the time your toddler enters school, writing reports will be something he or she understands how to do.

Writing a Group Story

Consider writing as a family! The family gathers together and decides on a story topic. Many times it is fun to write a story based on an event that actually happened, such as a family trip. Each family member writes a part of the story. If your preschooler does not yet write, let him or her dictate that portion of the story and you can write it down for your child. Children are excited to know that they helped create a story based on family history. Children feel ownership of the story and are always proud of what has been created, no matter how little or much they have contributed. This technique of "group writing" creates writing that is more colorful, more creative, and more complex than children could initially write on their own.

Keeping a Picture Journal or a Daily Journal

Writing something every day is the best way to get children into a writing habit. Younger children can write captions under drawn pictures, and beginning writers can be encouraged to write something daily about their experiences. These journals not only will be fun to read in later years but will document your child's growth as a writer. Once toddlers can talk in sentences, they can tell you about their day or a special event. As they talk, type on your computer or write out what they say. If they don't give you enough details, make certain to ask questions: What color was the dog? What was the weather like? Were you happy or sad? Don't worry about getting the facts correct in these journals. It is more important that children enjoy the writing and/or illustrating of their own stories.

Writing Letters

Authentic writing gives children a feeling of being real writers and should be encouraged whenever possible. Help your son or daughter write notes to friends and relatives or encourage them to include illustrated pictures in notes or cards you write. As a child gets older, he or she might be encouraged to maintain a writing correspondence with a pen pal or e-pal. Writing cards and letters on the computer make manipulating pictures and text even easier for young writers, and many sites encourage adding text to premade cards.

Encouraging Descriptions and Observations

If you go on a family trip or just take a daily car outing, encourage your child to talk about the things that he or she notices on the trip. Try to add to the description by encouraging the use of additional vocabulary words. (Was the tree tremendous? Was the park crowded? Were the animals frisky? What did the birds look like in the tree?) Children can draw detailed pictures of these sights and you can help them write about them.

Using Games and Puzzles

Games and puzzles not only encourage young children to read and speak but also prepare them for future writing tasks. Remember that these word and picture games build vocabulary, and a more expansive vocabulary makes for more expressive writing. Many crossword puzzles, word searches, word games, rhyming games, and even flash card games are designed especially for children and are available in book form or through a myriad of Internet Web sites.

Copying from Books or Poems

You can help your child create an early reading journal by helping him or her copy favorite lines or poems he or she already knows. If you bind the lines and poems, you will have created a book of favorite writings together. You can be sure that eventually your child will strive to imitate one of these favorite authors or poets and eventually begin composing some personal prose or verse.

Creating a Family Tree

Children can draw the tree and they can help write stories about the different individuals in the family. This endeavor, which could also be compiled in a "family album" format, can be fun for children of any age.

Dramatizing Stories

Drama is telling stories, and almost all children love to put on plays or puppet shows for the rest of the family. First, encourage them to create a storyboard of the presentation, using words or pictures. Invite children to tell what will happen first, then next, and then finally in conclusion. This planning step will help them create a better show and will get them started and excited about writing at the same time. You may wish to use the sample storyboard as a starting point.

Story title: *First Day at School*

Where the story takes place: *Smith Elementary School*

Characters: *Mary and Johnny*

Problem: *Mary is scared of her first day at school.*

What happens first: *Johnny rides on the bus with Mary.*

What happens next: *They get to school and the teacher meets them.*

What happens next: *The teacher invites them into the classroom.*

Solution: *Mary has fun all day and realizes school is a wonderful place.*

Setting a Good Example

Just as children need you to model reading for them, they also need to see you writing. In today's climate of endless television, computer games, and video entertainment, children don't always turn naturally to writing. If children perceive that writing is an enjoyable endeavor by seeing you do it, they will begin writing with enthusiasm, not dread. Look for writing opportunities that your child can do with you: writing out birthday or other invitations, making out grocery lists, or copying phone numbers into a book.

Parents of young children can help make writing easier by providing their writers with a place to write, the materials with which to write, and adequate time to spend thinking and writing. Just as students need a quiet place to study and a cozy nook to read, young writers need adequate lighting and a desk or table of the correct height for writing. These days many young students have access to computers and the Internet; it is equally important to have some kind of word processing software available to the child. In addition to the computer, you need to provide children with plenty of paper, pens or pencils, crayons, markers, and other materials with which to write and draw. Finally, time to think and plan is an essential writing tool, and your child should be encouraged to plan, to think, and to discuss ideas before writing. Remember to offer praise and encouragement no matter how the writing piece takes shape. A little encouragement will go a long way to having your child write again and again.

Elementary and Middle School Writers

The elementary and middle school child should continue with many of the creative writing tasks practiced as a younger writer. He or she can still keep a personal journal or diary, and should continue to write in it daily. Your child should also continue to write creatively: stories, plays, poems, and songs to be shared with friends and family. He or she can now independently sustain a pen pal relationship, by writing letters or e-mails to new or old friends.

THE WRITING PROCESS

Before you can help your child with his or her school writing, it is important to understand a few basic premises about the art of writing. Writing necessitates a series of steps or actions, and even skilled or experienced writers use this writing process to help them do their work. Although each writer works a little differently, all of them go through these steps as they create their written work. The writing process itself is recursive—that is to say that although writers visit each step of this process, they will often move back and forth through the various stages as they work. Writing does not happen in a straight line; rather, authors weave in and out of the steps before having something published.

As students enter school and begin writing in earnest, they should be encouraged to engage in the writing process to complete their assignments. The steps in the writing process are described below.

Prewriting: Prewriting is a beginning. This is the stage when the writer focuses on a chosen subject or topic, collects details by researching or generating ideas, decides on his or her audience and purpose, and decides what form the writing will take. Several prewriting activities will be discussed in the following pages.

Writing or Drafting: Drafting refers to the actual writing. The writer uses the ideas gathered in the prewriting phase and launches into writing the desired piece.

Revising: Revising occurs after the initial draft is complete. The author adds, deletes, rewrites, and reshapes any parts of the writing that are unclear or not concise. The author might even go back to either prewriting or writing/drafting if necessary.

Editing: Editing is the stage before publication. The writer rereads the text for mechanical errors in grammar, punctuation, spelling, or any other things needed to polish the writing. Note, however, that a writer can still go back at this point to any of the earlier stages if he or she does not think that the writing is ready for publication.

Publishing: In the writing process, publication refers to the sharing of the written work. For a student writer, publication may mean reading the piece aloud or displaying it on a bulletin board. In some classrooms, teachers have students bind their writings into book form, or they may staple several students' writings together in the same "publication." Sometimes, student writers find opportunities to really publish by sending their work to magazines, journals, newspapers, or even by posting it on the Internet.

Although the stages of the writing process are distinct, it is important to remember that the actual process is a different experience for every writer—furthermore, the process may even differ from work to work for the same writer. Sometimes a massive amount of research is required in the prewriting stage, while at other times much of the early work happens in the author's head or on little scraps of paper. Some works require much revision; others need very little editing. Despite these variables, most authors revisit a piece many times before submitting the completed text.

Writing simple facts about dinosaurs was fine for a basic pre-school report, but now your elementary or middle school student should be comfortable enough with reading and writing to write their own more complex reports. However, as with preschool report, you can take a role in the process; after all, much of the writing and research of school assignments will probably take place at home. The steps below will guide you through the writing process and give you some concrete strategies with which to help your child succeed.

WHAT SHOULD I WRITE ABOUT?

Often a teacher assigns a specific topic for school reports. There are other times, however, when students must choose their own topics. If your child consults you when deciding upon a writing topic, your advice should be simple: "Write about a subject that really interests you!" The interest factor can make all the difference in the quality of a student's writing. If a topic is exciting to your child, he or she will not mind spending time learning about that subject. The final product, when focused on a topic of personal interest, will usually be more descriptive, more colorful, and more expressive than if focused on a random theme of the teacher's (or your) choosing.

PREWRITING STRATEGIES

After receiving or deciding on the topic of a report, a student must learn how to limit or focus the broad topic. This is why the prewriting stage is key. This section explores some of the more common prewriting strategies that writers use to explore their ideas and limit their topics.

Free Writing

Free writing is a prewriting activity that helps many writers explore their thinking. Begin the free write with a sentence about the main topic. The idea is to write quickly and to find as many ideas as possible. Often, free writing helps writers find topics or thoughts that can be organized into compositions. For the new student writer, free writing should take about five minutes, no more. The student just keeps writing, with no attention to spelling or any other type of revising or editing. Sentence fragments are fine. Even single words can be repeated and repeated; the idea is to not lift the pen off the paper for the entire writing period. At the end of the writing session, your child will be amazed at some of the ideas that just "popped" onto the page.

Clustering

Another prewriting strategy taught to many students is an activity called clustering. (It is also known as mapping or webbing.) After selecting a topic of interest, students write it in the center of a piece of paper. They then branch off from that main word with other related words that occur to them. Clustering or mapping often leads in new directions and can uncover many interesting ideas about a given topic. Students should try to narrow their topics down and focus on specific details while clustering. Here is a sample cluster exercise using the word "pet."

Idea Listing

An idea listing is similar to clustering, but students simply write the topic at the top of a piece of paper and rapidly list any ideas they have about the topic. Sometimes students start with a cluster or idea list and then free write about the chosen topic.

Brainstorming

Brainstorming is an activity that usually takes place in a group setting. Students come up with thoughts, feelings, or ideas on a given topic and their ideas are recorded on the blackboard or on an overhead projector. Brainstorming is simply a way to generate ideas, so *all* ideas are recorded but none are analyzed or discussed during the session. Brainstorming, which produces numerous topics and is particularly effective with a large group, allows students to see a wide variety of perspectives on any one topic.

Rehearsing

Often, students find rehearsing an effective prewriting strategy. Rehearsing is simply discussing a topic before writing about it. If a student is at home, you can act as his or her partner. After your student shares his or her ideas about the topic, your job is to listen, to ask specific questions about the topic, and to point out anything that seems unclear. After receiving your reaction to the topic, the student may be better prepared to begin writing.

Narrowing the Topic

Learning to narrow the topic is one of the hardest endeavors for the beginning writer. Students need to remember that the main topic is usually far too broad a subject for one paper and that they need to focus the topic in order to make it manageable. Topics like "The Civil War," "Christopher Columbus," "The Environment," or "My Family" need to be honed down in order to write about them. Often the answer to the question, "How do I feel about X?" or "What do I want to say about X?" can be the one key sentence that effectively narrows the topic. For example, if the topic were "Cats," the student might ask, "How do I feel about cats?" The answer to that question (i.e., "Cats make wonderful pets.") will become the opening sentence in the paragraph. Look in the next section to find out more about a simple way to design a multi-paragraph essay.

Any of the prewriting strategies above can help narrow writing topics. In addition, considering the purpose and audience for the paper will often help the writer zero in on the main focus of the piece. It is imperative that students understand the purpose and audience before starting to write. A planning chart like the one that follows will help your child articulate why the paper is being written and what elements of the topic are most important. Remember, the overriding reason for writing anything is to *say something worth saying about something worth saying something about!*

WRITING PLANNING CHART

TOPIC _____

PURPOSE FOR WRITING (check off one or more that apply):

❏ To describe a person, a place or an object

❏ To explain how to do something

❏ To find out something about a topic

❏ To give an opinion

❏ To ask a question

❏ To persuade my audience

❏ To tell a true story

❏ To make up a story (fiction)

❏ Other

ABOUT THE READER:

1. Who will be reading this?

_____

2. What do I want to tell the reader about this topic?

_____

3. What part of this topic will interest the reader the most?

_____

Organizing Student Writing

Students are taught to organize their writing into paragraphs and then into a multi-paragraph essay. Essentially, the paragraph is a mini-essay, reflecting the basic construction of the essay itself. It begins with a topic sentence that tells what the paragraph is going to be about, includes a body that gives information to support that topic sentence, and ends with a closing sentence that in some way refers back to the topic sentence or main idea. For younger students, a good organizational device for writing paragraphs is a prewriting graphic organizer like the one below. Once all of the layers are filled in, the paragraph can be transferred to lined paper or to a word processing program.

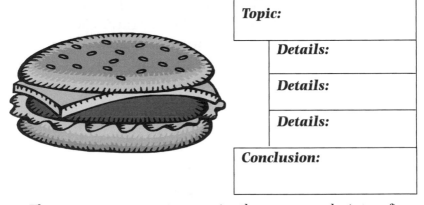

Topic:		
	Details:	
	Details:	
	Details:	
Conclusion:		

There are many ways to organize these paragraphs into a finished product, and good organization reflects clear thinking about the subject. One way to organize student papers or reports is to put the details in chronological order. (These papers are often organized using words like *first, second, third, finally*.) Another method is to organize the details in order of importance from the most important to the least important or vice versa. Yet a third organizational strategy is to state the main idea and then use details to illustrate the main idea. When writing a comparison, some students show how two things are alike and then move on to show how they are different. An overall design is needed if the paper is to be strong and flow logically.

Writing the first draft is the step after prewriting. Guided by the plan devised in the prewriting phase, the student now writes without worrying about making any mistakes. Revising is the process that happens after the first draft is complete. The piece is read and sentences are changed or rearranged in order to make the writing more concise. If some ideas are out of order, if not enough details are given, if some connections are unclear, the piece needs revision. Sometimes it will be necessary to go back and write more on the first draft, or do more prewriting research.

Only after the writer is satisfied that all revision has been executed is it time to edit the paper. Editing or proofreading is the final step before the paper is complete. This is the time to check for spelling and grammatical errors and to clean up other issues of syntax or punctuation. Many students find a writer's checklist helpful during the revising and editing process. There are many editing checklists available in books and on the Internet, but the following list will be helpful for a younger student.

WRITER'S CHECKLIST

Organization:

❑ Does the writing have a subject that is not too broad?

❑ Does the topic sentence name the subject and tell how you feel about it?

❑ Is the writing well organized? Does it have a beginning, a middle, and an end?

❑ Are all your ideas arranged in the best order?

Details:

❑ Does the writing include supporting details?

WRITER'S CHECKLIST (cont.)

❑ Does the writing support your opinions with reasons and details?

Style:

❑ Is the writing easy to understand?

❑ Is everything clear to the reader?

Mechanics:

❑ Has the writing been checked for spelling errors?

❑ Has the writing been checked for complete sentences?

❑ Has the writing been checked for punctuation?

 High School Writers

By the time your son or daughter reaches high school, he or she has been exposed to a number of different forms of writing. Listed below are some of the types of writing that students have encountered or practiced in their prior schooling experience:

Autobiographies

Biographies

Book Reviews/Book Reports

Descriptions

Editorials

E-mail

Essays

Explanations

Fictional Writing

Historical Writing

Interviews

Journals

Myths

News Stories

Personal Letters

Plays

Poems

Reports

Short Stories

Songs

Reflections

To succeed in high school and college, your child will have to employ very specific writing skills: the short answer response for use on tests, the essay format for longer papers, and the organization of a formal research paper. The student will find that with practice each type of writing will become easier and easier.

THE SHORT ANSWER RESPONSE

High school tests in every discipline often ask for short answer responses to given questions. Many high-stakes tests call this kind of question an open-ended response question. This is not a multiple-choice question, nor is it a fill-in-the-blank, one word response. Rather, it is a question that asks the student to carefully consider a particular question and to construct a thoughtful, written, analytical response. Often, this type of question has several parts to which the student must respond; credit is reduced if a student does not answer every part of the question. Here are a few examples of short answer questions in various disciplines:

- **English:** Dialogue is an important element of the story you just read. Identify which two characters' dialogues sound the most realistic. Describe the effect the story might have if the author had not used regional diction.

- **Science:** From the article we read on the ozone layer, summarize the three ideas that support the author's main purpose. What plan might you propose if the National Academy of Science asked you for a solution to the ozone problem?

- **Social Studies:** According to the following article, the average person in the United States is subjected to thousands of advertisements every week. Compare and contrast the author's feeling that advertisements are a way of life in America with your own perception of this same issue.

Strategies for Short Answers

There are several specific strategies for answering this type of question. The student must be aware that since this is a timed writing task, the teacher or grader is *not* looking for a polished, flawless piece of writing. Rather, the questions are constructed to assess student understanding of the given content and application to other subjects or to the student's general knowledge. The writing must be clear, well organized, analytic, and should usually refer back to the given text for support and details.

Step One:

The first step in answering the open-ended question is to understand precisely what the question is asking. Students must read the question slowly and carefully. Students should be trained to look for and circle key words that will help them focus their essay and will explain the required task. Here is a selection of common key words with which students should be familiar:

Identify: This means answering the "5 W's" about a subject: Who? What? Where? When? Why?

Compare: Explain how things are alike.

Contrast: Explain how things are different. (Note that some questions may ask students to compare and contrast a subject.)

Explain: Discuss what something means or how or why it works.

Summarize: Extrapolate the important information about a given text.

Analyze: Break down the given information into parts in order to clearly examine it.

List: Give a specific number of examples or details.

Prove: Provide facts and details to show something is true.

Evaluate: Express an opinion about something by highlighting the positive and negative points. It also must be supported by facts and details.

Step Two:

The student should use the order of the question as a plan for organizing the writing. In a timed piece of writing, it is helpful to answer the question(s) in the order it is written.

Step Three:

The student should use a scrap piece of paper, or the back of the exam if it is allowed, and take the next few minutes to write out the introductory paragraph or the topic sentence. On an open-ended question there is no need to take the time to restate the question itself. A student should just begin his or her focused answer.

Step Four:

Another minute or two should be spent jotting down some of the major ideas that will be included in the response. This can be done with a word map, a web, or just with a list of words. Remember that the focus must respond to exactly what the question has asked. One or two sentences usually suffice for a conclusion for this type of writing. The open-ended response can be one or more paragraphs.

Step Five:

After writing the response, the student should go back and check that he or she answered every detail of the question. For example, if the question asked for *characters* or *reasons*, then the response should include more than one character or more than one reason. If possible, the student should reread the answer once more for clarity and for any obvious mechanical or spelling errors.

Length of the Short Answer

Sometimes, students elect to write one paragraph for each part of the question and one paragraph for the conclusion. The length for this type of writing is not nearly as important as the organization and the supporting details from the text or from the student's knowledge of the subject. The reader wants to know that the student has understood the question, answered it with the correct information, and extended his or her understanding through some type of application.

THE FORMAL ESSAY

Even more common in high school than the short answer response, is an essay assignment about a particular topic. Sometimes this type of writing is termed the five-paragraph essay or the thesis composition. Some students find this particular assignment quite easy, while others claim that this is the hardest type of writing to do. Many students find it easiest to get started on their essay writing when they use the organizer shown on the following page. It trains students to focus their writing and makes the organization of the essay foolproof. It also guarantees the use of details and examples to prove the main thesis. This easy, step-by-step method for composing the five-paragraph essay is a technique that provides your child a visual image of how a paper should be properly developed.

An Organizational
List for Essay Writing

1. State the **topic**. (The topic can also be the title of your paper.)

2. For whom am I writing this paper? (Be as specific as possible about your **audience** and keep it in mind as you write.)

3. Ask yourself: How do I feel about the topic? Write one sentence that describes what you think about this subject. Remember to be specific and do not be indecisive! (This becomes your **thesis sentence** and part of the introductory paragraph (paragraph #1) of your paper.)

4. Ask yourself: How am I going to **prove my point** to the reader? Write two or three sentences in which you state three reasons for the stand which you have taken. Prove your point to the reader. These become **the additional sentences in paragraph #1.**

5. For the first reason you have written in paragraph #1, write down two or three facts, examples, or specific details that support your opinion. These become **paragraph #2.**

6. For the second reason you have written in paragraph #1, write down two or three facts, examples, or specific details that support your opinion. These become **paragraph #3.**

7. For the third reason you have written in paragraph #1, write down two or three facts, examples, or specific details that support your opinion. These become **paragraph #4.**

8. Write at least two sentences that summarize what you have said in your paper and that restate your thesis from the (introductory) paragraph. These become **paragraph #5.**

Here is how this graphic organizer will look when used for a real topic. We will use a simple subject to illustrate how this organizer works.

Topic:	Cats
AUDIENCE:	*Teacher and classmates*
Question: (How do I feel about this topic?):	**Sentence #1, paragraph #1**: Cats make wonderful pets. (Thesis statement) (Note: There is no doubt how the author feels about cats.)
Question: (How am I going to prove this to my reader?):	**Sentence #2, paragraph #1:** Cats are easy to train with very little effort. **Sentence #3, paragraph #1:** Most cats are inexpensive to maintain. **Sentence #4, paragraph #1:** Cats are independent which makes care easy for the owner.
Paragraph #2 (Examples to support sentence #2, paragraph #1.) (How am I going to prove that "cats are easy to train with very little effort"?)	My aunt once had a cat that she trained in two days! She only had to put down a little milk in the saucer and the cat learned to come running into the kitchen. When my neighbor's cat hears a little dinner bell, he comes running to the front porch. Our cat, Jinx, has quickly learned to roll over on command!

Topic:	Cats
AUDIENCE:	*Teacher and classmates*
Paragraph #3 (Examples to support sentence # 3, paragraph # 1) (How am I going to prove that "most cats are easy to maintain?")	The first time we got a kitten, we found an old basket and a warm blanket. This became her new bed. She was so tiny that a small saucer of milk and a little cat food was all she required. Our cat was so clean and she completely groomed herself!
Paragraph # 4 (Examples to support sentence #4, paragraph #1) (How am I going to prove that "most cats are independent?")	Cats can be left alone for longer periods of time than most other animals. As long as they have food and water they can amuse themselves. Unlike dogs, cats do not need to be taken on long walks in freezing cold weather. A cat knows when it wants to eat, sleep, or even be petted!
Paragraph #5 (Conclusion)	Even if one is a novice pet owner, it is very easy to care for a cat. They basically train themselves because they are so smart, and they cost very little in housing or care. Furthermore, their independent natures make them a breeze to raise. Cats make the world's best pets, as any cat owner will happily report.

It is now very easy for your child to take this information and write it out in paragraph form. Yes, this is a very basic scaffold for an essay paper. After the student becomes comfortable with these basics, he or she can refine the process by beginning the opening paragraph with a "hook," an interesting statement that gets the reader's attention. The opening sentence might also start with a surprising fact, an interesting description, or an intriguing question. More advanced writers might use quotations or anecdotes to help prove their main thesis. Closing paragraphs can also be more sophisticated, and perhaps pose a question for final study or end on a startling note. These are all techniques that will be refined as writers become more adept with the essay form.

This basic format can be used for your child's longer papers, too. They simply need to elaborate more in the introduction, add many more supporting details or examples, and tie everything together in the conclusion. In fact, most research formulas follow this same general format: The author explains what he or she is going to prove or demonstrate, the body paragraphs go about proving that thesis, and the concluding paragraphs revisit the proofs and summarize what the paper had attempted to illustrate or illuminate.

NOTE TAKING IN HIGH SCHOOL

High school students will be required, on an almost daily basis, to do an important, but informal kind of writing: taking notes. In addition to reading textbooks, listening to teachers, and participating in class discussions, writing excellent notes is an important skill that can help your child excel. For many students, however, note taking is a dreary chore that yields very little return for the effort. Basically, this is because so many of them do not know how to take efficient notes—some students write down everything a teacher says, while others have disorganized notes that make little sense. Used correctly, notes can help your son or daughter focus attention, remember content information, and gain a deeper understanding of the material. Note taking is an individual endeavor and no two students do it quite the same way. However, just like the writing organizer helps students *learn* how to write an essay, specific strategies exist to help students *learn* to take effective notes. After gaining proficiency with one method, students can then customize the method to make it their own.

Taking Lecture Notes

Encourage your son or daughter to use a three-ring binder for class notes since it allows them to add or remove pages as necessary.

Advise them to take notes on only one side of each page for the same reason. One very effective method for recording classroom information is the *Cornell Note-Taking Method.* With this system, the lined page is divided into three parts as shown below:

CORNELL NOTE-TAKING FORMAT

Subject: _____ Date: _____	
Main Ideas	**Details**
Summary:	

Information from the lecture is recorded in the larger portion on the right side of the page. The left portion is kept blank, as is the bottom of the page. After taking notes, the student goes home and reviews them. The "main ideas" are then listed in the column on the left. The student also summarizes the lecture in the portion on the bottom. Reviewing the initial notes as soon as possible after the class lecture makes it easy to remember the information. Identifying the main ideas helps clarify the information, and writing a summary makes studying much easier in later weeks. When the student is ready to study for a test, he or she vertically folds the sheet of paper, leaving only the main ideas visible. He or she then tries to recite all that can be remembered about the topic. If there is a problem, the notes can be checked by turning over the paper. Sometimes it is helpful for your child to recite the recorded facts to you; you can then offer prompts if important details are forgotten.

Here are some important tips that students should remember while taking those right-hand column notes:

- Date and number each page. This will help later with organization.

- Listen carefully. That sounds pretty simple, but if the mind wanders during a lecture, important points will be lost and crucial clues might be missed. For example, when the topic is introduced the teacher will often announce what the focus of the lesson is going to be. "Today we are going to learn the three rules for...." The student who hears this statement knows which important points in the lecture to focus on.

- Don't write down everything the teacher says. Complete sentences are a waste of time in note taking. Use abbreviations for certain words and use only key words in sentences. "Act I—multiple foreshadowing" is enough to remember that "In Act I, Macbeth receives multiple foreshadowings of things to come."

Don't worry about spelling. If a word is new, the student should just attempt a phonetic spelling for now.

Do not worry at all about correct punctuation.

Underline things that are given considerable emphasis, or that are repeated over and over.

Listen for key words such as, *first, second, finally, most important, as a result,* and *consequently.* Most teachers use these words to organize their lectures.

Include any handouts in the notes, and record anything that has been written on the board on an overhead.

Taking Reading Notes

Taking reading notes has been explained at length in Chapter One. In particular, you may find it helpful to review the explanation of the SQ3R method. Reading notes are even easier to take than lecture notes, as there is more time to review the text while one is reading. However, here are a few helpful tips your son or daughter should remember during reading assignments.

Preview any assignment before reading. Read any charts, graphs, picture or illustration captions, and all headings and subheadings.

Read for answers to questions—questions that have come from the headings and subheadings.

If permitted, use a highlighter over key phrases or ideas that may need to be remembered. Likewise, margin notes can also be a helpful tool for later review.

When reviewing, also highlight important notes you have written about the text.

Write down any questions about the reading to get clarification from the teacher or through further research.

SOME FINAL IDEAS FOR HIGH SCHOOL WRITERS

Writing is all about practice, practice, practice. The more one writes, the better writer one becomes. High school students can get lots of practice by writing regularly in a journal. Journals can be vehicles for expressing oneself, such as with a private diary. There are, however, other types of journals appropriate for high school writers. In journals known as "Learning Logs," for example, students record information learned and connections made among the subjects they are studying at school. There are also "Reader Response Journals" in which readers record reactions and feelings about books that they have studied. This type of journal is often used in English classes in high school. A "Dialogue Journal" is one in which the student and a friend, teacher, or relative write back and forth to one another. Dialogue journals often help young people express emotions and examine important situations.

Many students find that keeping a file of "Writing Ideas" is a helpful way to gather inspiration for future writings. They can simply keep a small book or journal and jot down details about memorable scenes, interesting events, people encountered, important places visited, or even a dream that they have had. Students should add to this kind of journal on a routine basis, and can even include clipped articles from magazines or newspapers, collected recipes, photos taken, or virtually anything that might become material for a piece of writing one day.

3

CREATING EXCITEMENT ABOUT SCHOOL

Enthusiasm and excitement about school carries over from day to day and from subject to subject.
— Anonymous

A s a parent, you will have an enormous impact on your child's attitude about school as well as on his or her performance in class. Not only should you support and encourage the learning that occurs in school, but you need to stay involved in your son or daughter's "life" in school. Schools need you to be a partner in your child's learning experiences if those experiences are to be maximized. There will be some specific ways to do that in Chapter 4: Attending Back-to-School Night.

To get your child enthusiastic about school, you may very well need to leave behind your own residual feelings about school. Saying things like "I hated math, too," or "You are going to have homework for the rest of your life," serve no purpose and can only produce negative feelings about the school experience. You need to be upbeat, involved, and positive, and help your child's teachers do their job of encouraging children to become responsible for their own learning. What follows are some specific actions you can take to make this happen.

Preschool, Kindergarten, and Younger Elementary School Learners

PLAYING SCHOOL

Playing "school" is a natural pastime for preschool children, especially if they have older brothers or sisters. Parents should arrange to have a special place—a desk, a table, or some other special nook—that can be used as a schoolroom. There should be plenty of crayons, pencils, paper, coloring books, alphabet letters, and numbers available for your child to use. There are even mini-chalkboards and magnetic letter boards available for purchase. Children should also have access to scissors and old magazines or newspapers, some school glue and tape, and other artistic tools, if possible. The more entertaining you make this area, the easier it will be for your child to get the message that school can be fun. Naturally, there should also be plenty of children's books within reach. Reinforce this fun time by praising your children and by explaining that they are learning just like they will in school when they get older. Playing school should never lead to anger or frustration; some children will be ready for this type of play and others may have to wait until they are a little older. However, the most important thing is that "school" is presented as a stress-free, feel-good kind of playtime.

GETTING OFF TO A GOOD START

A wonderful summer is over and it is your child's first day at school. Whether it is the first day of kindergarten or your child is returning to another year of school, this should be a very exciting day, and one that should be anticipated for days or weeks. The first day of a new academic year is a new beginning. Your son or daughter will be going into a new class, with the possibility of making new friends and learning new knowledge. He or she should go off that first day with a clean, empty backpack, a notebook and an assignment pad, several sharpened pencils or new pens, and a smile on his or her face. Everything should have your child's name printed in a prominent place so that his or her possessions can be easily identified. It will also be helpful, before that first day, for you to discuss what may happen. Mention that the teacher is likely to send home information, and tell your child where to place those notices. Sometimes, a pocket folder can be used expressly for this purpose. Another folder can be supplied for your child's work in school; keeping the work in a folder or special place will send the message that you value schoolwork and want to keep it neat and clean. Explain the use of an assignment pad, and have your child practice writing in it. All of these early expectations may not be met, but initial discussions can help your child realize the importance of being organized and will set patterns for later in the year.

GETTING ORGANIZED

It is important to remember that the goal of schooling is to make students lifelong learners. This happens by teaching learning and study skills that help students acquire new knowledge and process new information. Indeed, students learn many of these skills from the day they are born. Listening, understanding directions, managing time, problem solving, and setting goals are the focus of day-to-day lessons encountered by preschool children. As these same children enter school, these skills are called further into play as the children are exposed to more complicated information, become more socially active, and begin to compete with themselves and others to meet high expectations. At this point, students need to practice these known skills and acquire some others so that they can begin to take responsibility for their own learning. As students gather more and more study and learning skills, they learn to handle increasingly rigorous academic challenges with greater success.

Elementary and Middle School Learners

Elementary students feel pride as they become more independent learners. It is still imperative, however, that you remain closely attuned to what is happening at school. When your child returns home from school, you or the assigned caregiver should sit down for a few minutes with him or her and discuss the day's events. It is equally important to go through your child's backpack and/or notebook to check for any notices or papers that have been sent home. Elementary teachers are famous for sending notes home; these same notes could stay in the backpack a week or longer if you don't think to empty it!

Take some time to review any schoolwork that has made it home, and inquire if there is any homework assigned. If there is homework, check to see that your child recorded it in his or her assignment pad. The assignment notebook can even help you keep in touch with what is being taught, and keep you informed about any assignments that are due or tests or quizzes for which to prepare. It may seem too early in a child's education to insist upon this organizational tool, but the sooner he or she learns to write down this type of information, the sooner he or she will be on the path to academic success. Organization is one of the key elements that separates students who excel from those who do not. Teachers, especially in elementary and middle schools, often remind young students to record their homework in an assignment pad. In fact, many schools now provide students with assignment books or agendas. If the school does not yet do this, you might wish to suggest it at a PTA meeting. When your child comes home and completes his or her work, you can make certain that the assignment is checked off or initialed to show that it is finished. Parents can serve as important role models by sharing with children their own systems for staying organized: Notepads, lists, electronic schedules, or family calendars all show that this activity is something that grownups also find necessary.

TIME MANAGEMENT STRATEGIES

Time management is another skill that is essential for student success. Like organizational skills, this is also a skill that must begin early in order to set patterns for future academic success. Students do not need to spend endless hours to study efficiently. Using time wisely, eliminating major distractions, and studying in a specific, comfortable location can make study time much more pleasant and infinitely more productive. Homework and study time should be a scheduled event; although the precise time will depend on your child's age and bedtime, homework should always be done before he or she is too tired to think clearly. Some find it convenient to have homework completed before dinner, leaving the evening free for television or personal activities. Others find that relaxation time after school is essential and that some children are more focused after dinner. This is certainly a personal decision that only you can make for your own children. The point is that some amount of study time should be set aside every evening—even if it is only to review notes taken in class, or for reading an outside book. This might also be a wonderful time for your child to record something in a personal journal in order to enhance writing skills and encourage reflective thinking.

THE OPTIMAL STUDY SPACE

Many young children want to begin doing their homework on the kitchen table, right in the midst of the family hubbub. This is perfectly natural, for students don't want to feel like they are missing out on all the fun while they are sequestered and studying. By sitting with the family, youngsters are also closer to mom, dad, big brother, or big sister, who can readily lend a hand with homework.

Don't let children get into this habit and you won't have to break them of it later. Instead, provide a purposefully quiet and comfortable atmosphere and their studying will produce results that make you both proud. The following are some guidelines for creating the right atmosphere for good study habits for students of every age. Training students, beginning in the earliest grades, to organize materials and work space will help support study efforts later in the schooling process. By teaching study skills at an early age, students have the opportunity to practice and refine these skills as their education becomes more rigorous and demanding.

Creating a Study Space

1. Select a quiet place that has minimal distractions and where your child will not be continuously interrupted. This may be your child's room or a separate study or library. It can even be a small corner designed with the proper study equipment in mind. The television, the telephone, or sometimes loud music can all distract a child who is studying. (Some children find that certain types of music actually help them to focus. The key here is that the sounds not be distracting, but rather a "background" stimulus.) Sometimes even a computer loaded with games or instant messaging can distract students from their primary study focus. Have your child use the same place to study on a routine basis. This will help him or her develop a regular study routine.

2. Provide your child with a desk, table, or other flat surface that has room for spreading out books and writing materials. The chair should be comfortable, with a straight or almost straight back. This has been found to be the best posture for reading and studying. Reading on a bed or lying on the floor can hurt concentration and make a child sleepy.

3. Make certain that there is good lighting in the study area. The aim is to provide adequate lighting without glare so that eye

fatigue is kept to a minimum. Natural lighting is wonderful where and when available, and there are now many lamps and lightbulbs available that closely approximate natural lighting.

4. Provide a study area that is free from clutter. Keeping a study area tidy, with supplies neatly stored and easily accessible, helps students stay organized and eliminates wasted time searching for correct materials.

5. Help your child set up a basic filing system. Throughout a school year, students bring papers and supplies back and forth from school to home and vice versa. It is important that students periodically "weed out" those papers and notes they won't need; it is equally important that students put important papers in a safe place so that they can study for subsequent tests by using prior notes and information.

6. Temperature control is important in creating an ideal study situation. The study space should be neither too cold nor too warm. Temperatures that are too warm or too cold can impede proper focus, and can make children sleepy or distracted.

7. Be aware that periodic study breaks can help students refocus and can actually produce more efficient study time. If a child has been doing homework for several hours, this is probably a sign that he or she is too distracted or is not working to the fullest capacity. It is quite possibly time for a study break!

About Learning Styles

In the past several years, educational researchers have uncovered much information about individual learning styles. Learning style is the way in which someone best absorbs information. There are a wide variety of learning styles, and some people have mixed styles. There is not any one best learning style; it is a highly individualized preference and any style can be as effective as another, given that a person knows and understands his own needs and preferences. All learning styles have strengths and weaknesses, but knowing which one your child has can yield important information about the way to approach studying.

Some people learn best by seeing information; these are visual learners. Others learn best by hearing information; these are auditory learners. Still others are kinesthetic learners, which means that they learn best by moving their bodies to learn—through dramatic presentation, for example. Of course, most people use more than one of their senses when they learn.

Besides these learning styles, there are many other ways that learning preferences come into play. Some people learn best in a routine method, while others do not mind information delivered in a random fashion. Some of us like to see the outcome before exploring the individual parts, while others like to work up to the "big picture." It is important to realize that although a person may prefer one particular method of learning, he or she can still learn about and improve in other methods. Indeed, the development of learning styles is an important goal of education.

How can you determine your child's particular learning style? Start with your computer. Many sites on the Internet offer free "Learning Styles" surveys. These usually consist of a number of statements about learning that together offer a composite picture of a particular learning style. It might be fun for you and your child to take one of these surveys and to discuss your preferences. This activity can assist you as you develop a blueprint for helping your child study. It may even provide guidance as you plan the design of an appropriate study space for him or her.

Knowledge of one's learning style can also be helpful for schoolwork. If you realize that your child is a visual learner, for example, it will be helpful to enhance a history lesson with pictures, graphs, maps, charts, or timelines as study guides. If a child is an auditory learner, it may be helpful to hear explanations after attempting a reading.

THINKING POSITIVELY

No matter which learning style is used, positive visualization is imperative if young learners are to do well in school. This is an area where parents can be indispensable. Worry or feelings of inadequacy can interfere with a student's self-image as well as his or her ability to learn. Students need reinforcement and commendations; positive feedback on study efforts and schoolwork will lead to a student feeling that he or she can succeed. Encouraging and working with youngsters to set goals is an excellent way to get them excited about school and the challenges of education. Success breeds success, and enthusiasm can go a long way to making youngsters competent and responsible learners. As students develop winning attitudes, they will make sacrifices and do what it takes to continue to believe in themselves.

 High School Learners

Although most teenagers would vehemently deny it, high school students also need parents involved in their educational process. This involvement, however, should happen in a subtle way; parents must use a bit of psychology to stay in touch with their high school age child.

By the time a child reaches high school, he or she feels independent and in no need of help from mom or dad. Questions like "What happened in school today?" will more often than not be answered with "Nothing." Homework inquiries may be dismissed by "I don't have any," or "I did it in school."

In some ways, this is exactly the way things should be. Both parents and teachers want adolescents to become responsible and accountable for their own learning. On the other hand, many teens are trying out their freedom and independence for the first time, and feel resistant to parental involvement or what they perceive to be interference in their lives. With so many other pressures on the teen learner, study skills or educational goals often get tabled. What teens consider to be more important pursuits—the telephone, computer, sports activities, clubs, social arrangements, music, the latest fashions, part-time jobs, movies, television, and a million other of life's intrusions—can distract them from their primary goal of learning and doing well in school. Sometimes, the long-term goals of college or future jobs are not enough of a motivation to sustain interest in further education.

THE GOOD NEWS

Students who have earlier established a winning attitude and positive feelings about school will most often continue to have those feelings in high school. Likewise, study habits that have been learned and honed in students' younger years will most probably be carried forward through their teens. And you, as parent, can certainly help reinforce positive images, sustain excitement about schooling, and help motivate students to improve academic performance.

How do the parents of high schoolers keep their children enthusiastic about school? First, parents can help students develop or maintain good study habits by providing the materials, space, and scheduled time for studying to occur. Next, communication with the school and an understanding of the programs the school offers can make parents aware of educational goals and the resources available to help students in need. What follows are some specific tips for parents on supporting student learning—keeping these guidelines in mind will keep your son or daughter from falling into poor performance patterns.

GOAL SETTING

Many high school students have vague goals and no clear direction for achieving their dreams. Sometimes, the goals they do have are so long-term (eventual careers, monetary gain, graduate education) that they find it difficult to sustain the motivation required to realize these outcomes. Young people need help to set clear, realistic goals with specific intermediate steps so that they can follow through and feel successful about themselves along the way. It is important to discuss goals with your child and help him or her understand how to realize them. Make certain to distinguish between long- and short-term goals; achieving short-term goals will help develop those patterns of behavior that lead to other successes. If a child feels ownership of the set goals—meaning that he or she desires them on his or her own—the hard work required to achieve these goals will come naturally. Goals should be linked with action, and your child should understand that goals are based on "if/then thinking." ("If I do X, then Y will happen.")

Help your child set both short-term and long-term academic goals. For example, if a child wants to earn a high grade in a particular subject, let's say French, look at the length of time needed to achieve that long-term goal. Most marking periods are ten weeks long; encourage your son or daughter to break that period into smaller chunks of time with specific goals attached to each portion of time. By writing down his or her specific goals, your child can see the actual steps required to achieve success. The goal for week one might be "study French during my study hall period," or perhaps, "study French verbs for fifteen minutes every night." Week two's goals might be to "practice French for one hour every Tuesday and Thursday," and so forth, until the ultimate goal of the higher grade is met. Remember that the hardest part of setting a goal is staying on task; you can help your student by encouraging him or her to remain focused. Do not, however, constantly badger your child about the goal; you do not want this to become a confrontational experience. Goal-setting, when done properly, is simply a way to focus the adolescent and help him or her feel good about learning.

SETTING PRIORITIES AND
TIME MANAGEMENT

Learning to set priorities is another important aspect of goal setting and one that becomes more complex with maturity. A priority is something your child wants to do: go to the movies, watch television, go out with his or her friends, have a sleep-over party. Setting priorities is part of the learning process and intricately tied to setting goals. You need to teach your child how to evaluate desires—what he or she would like to do—against the goal that he or she has committed to. If doing homework and talking on the phone are conflicts, help your child understand which is more important and which will eventually help achieve a particular goal. Students can learn to use the things they want to do as rewards for accomplishing their goals. ("If I get an "A" in French, I will go see a movie.") Again, if the goal is short-term, success can be achieved in a shorter time. Once success is achieved, the student will want to feel that great feeling again and again.

High school students, not unlike their younger counterparts, need your help to manage their time. Provide your son or daughter with an agenda book or an electronic calendar so that they can keep track of assignments and visually be reminded of important due dates for projects and tests. Many high school students do no think an assignment pad is "cool" and try to keep track of everything in their heads. Obviously, this is not feasible, since students in high school have assignments from five, six, or even more subjects to remember throughout a given day. Ask students to see their notebooks or show you what they have for homework; this is a wonderful way for you to stay connected with what is happening daily at school.

As students advance in school, there are many more demands on their time, and much more independent work is required of them. This is wonderful preparation for college, when professors give assignments and expect much of the work to be done outside of class. During the high school years, students are given a number of long-term projects that necessitate scheduling time to complete. Unit tests or writing tasks are familiar assignments that take days or sometimes weeks to complete correctly. Many students procrastinate on these kinds of assignments because of fear of failure or, more often, because of lack of organizational and time-management skills. These assignments, however, should be given high priority, since many subject areas heavily weigh them for marking period grades. Again, if you can help a student break down the long-term assignment into smaller chunks, there will be enough time to do an adequate job with the task. Remember that you are there to support and encourage your child, not to do the work for him or her. Making mistakes and failing to meet timed tasks, to some degree, can be important learning experiences. After a scholastic setback, your job is to make certain the child picks himself or herself up again and help explain how using certain study skills could have improved his or her performance. Just pointing out what the child did wrong or admonishing him or her to try harder the next time is not an effective approach and does not give your child enough ownership of the learning process. Help your child come to his or her own understanding of what went wrong.

STUDY SKILLS

It is well known that the ultimate understanding of a particular task is manifested in one's ability to teach it to another. Study time, particularly in the high school years, can easily become a time when you learn from your child! Many parents help students study by rote drilling and repetition of facts. Instead, consider having your son or daughter teach *you* the test material. Let him or her explain *why* the Americans won the Revolutionary War, or *how* weather is a predictor of certain disasters. Or ask your child to defend the actions of a particular literary figure. Learn to ask your child questions that require critical thinking about the material; this type of studying/learning promotes authentic understanding of the content. A critical aspect of this type of studying is that students comprehend that learning is lifelong; in a community of learners we all can learn from one another. There are a number of other test-taking skills discussed later in this book.

LIFE OUTSIDE THE CLASSROOM

An important component to the high school experience is your son or daughter's involvement with extracurricular activities. These can include sports activities, drama clubs, chorus or band clubs, cheerleading, class-specific activities, honors clubs, yearbook, journalism, or art activities. In fact, the list is endless. These pursuits become a major factor in your child's social adjustment to high school and are important for maintaining excitement about school. In addition, they are often a source for high school friendships and the basis for building peer groups. Despite what verbal messages high school students may send, they really do want parents involved in their schooling. There are many ways this can and should happen. Most important, it is crucial for you to attend activity-sponsored events. Sporting games, dramatic presentations, and academic awards ceremonies, are all vehicles for telling your child, "I'm proud of you." and "Keep up the good work!" Furthermore, your presence sends the message that what your child is doing is important and worthy of his or her (and your) time and effort. It will also give you the opportunity to connect with other parents and school personnel, all of whom can help you understand and access the school's resources.

If you are excited about your child's accomplishments, both inside and outside the classroom, it will unfailingly get him or her excited as well. A child's school life is the most important thing he or she does for twelve or thirteen years of life. Patterns and expectations set early will set the tone for many, many years ahead. Supporting your child's learning with enthusiasm can be one of the greatest gifts you can give your son or daughter. Providing the tools they need to succeed in school will give the reinforcement needed to extend academic instruction into lifelong learning skills and to create a positive self-image so critical for adult achievement.

4

ATTENDING BACK-TO-SCHOOL NIGHT

As parents journey back-to-school, they bring with them the joys, the fears, the excitement that they themselves experienced therein.
—Anonymous

Back-to-School Night can be one of the most important events of the school year for both elementary and secondary parents. Most schools host this evening shortly after the beginning of the year so that a home–school foundation can start early enough to make a difference in a child's educational progress. You should watch for a flyer or other public announcement late in August or early in September that gives you the time and date of the planned event. Be sure to mark it on your calendar and make whatever arrangements necessary for transportation or babysitting. If you only attend one event at school all year (although this is not advised) be certain it is this one. Unfortunately, for numerous reasons, many parents do not participate in this most pivotal evening. And, among those who do attend, many do not use the information gained to maximize the school-year experience. To fully appreciate this evening, it is helpful to understand what schools and teachers hope to accomplish and the type of information you should expect to obtain.

WHAT TO EXPECT

Schools normally schedule this event in the evening hours during the school week. It usually takes place within the first six weeks of school. The schools are cleaned up after school, teachers and administrators go home to freshen up and return at a specified time to meet parents. Typically, the evening begins with a whole-group presentation in the space at your school that holds the most people, generally the auditorium or gymnasium. The superintendent, the principal, or another administrator usually gives an overview of the evening and of the school year. Leaders of the parent organization usually address the audience and describe some of the activities and fundraisers planned for the year. Often, videos are presented to highlight events of the past year or two. Don't forget: *you* are the student tonight, so be prepared to take notes on all the information you will be receiving! Also arrive prepared to sign up for any parent groups, as they will keep you actively involved in your child's school life. Parental involvement helps students achieve more and helps build quality schools for our communities.

You will usually receive a sheet of paper with your son's or daughter's class schedule. It shows the period, the teacher, and the room number for the class. There may be a school map attached, so you can easily find your way around the building. After the group session, you will often be given a tour of the school; sometimes this is done by students selected especially for this honor. You will get to see an overview of the facilities and really have an opportunity to experience your son's or daughter's daily world.

Typically, the rest of the evening will be spent with your child's teacher or teachers. A bell or announcement will usually herald the beginning of the first class. Parents spend anywhere from ten to twenty minutes in the child's classroom. You will sit at the students' desks; younger students will often have prepared the room and labeled their desk in some way so that you can sit in your own child's chair. The teacher may pass out a sign-in sheet so that he or she can match parents with the correct face or have an idea of which parents attended the evening.

Once everyone is in the room, your child's teacher will introduce herself or himself and begin speaking about the class. Back-to-School Night is an opportunity for the instructional staff to do the following:

- Underscore his or her high expectations for student achievement.

- Highlight course content as well as the state standards that align with that content.

- Provide examples of classroom activities that enhance and facilitate the teaching/learning process.

- Give an overview of daily routines and class schedule.

- Provide information on the assessment process.

- Establish a basis for future dialogue with parents.

- Discuss the homework policy, including assignments, amount of time to be spent on homework, submission regulations, and grading policy.

- Outline his or her discipline policy and measures taken to uphold that policy.

- Discuss the books he or she intends to use for the year and let you examine them in closer detail.

- Review the ways to communicate between home and school: telephone, e-mail, Web site information, or letters.

- Explain how to set up an appointment to discuss individual students or to address any specialized concerns that parents may have.

YOUR ROLE AS PARENT

For your part, there are certain things that you should remember to do while sitting in your child's classroom on Back-to-School Night. For example:

- Introduce yourself to the teacher either on the way in or on the way out of the classroom.

- Look around the classroom to get some clues about the environment. Is it a warm, inviting place with student work prominently and proudly displayed? Are there motivational posters or other artwork on the walls? Is there a specific place that homework and notices are displayed?

- Notice whether there are hours posted for extra help. If so, write the times down so you can urge your child to take advantage of this service when necessary.

- Note any contact information that the teacher gives you: a phone number, an e-mail address, a Web page, or other ways to connect. Make certain to write down this information somewhere where you will not lose it!

- Listen carefully to the teacher's description of his or her expectations and daily observations.

- Understand the homework policy of each teacher. (It may differ from teacher to teacher.)

- Understand other assessment tools the teacher will use to evaluate your son or daughter.

- Understand how you can work with your son or daughter to support student achievement.

- Make sure you are clear on what students in this class should know or be able to do by the end of the marking period and by the end of the year.

- Feel free to ask general questions about the specific class; however, remember that this is not the appropriate time to discuss individual students. You can make a later appointment to have a parent–teacher conference about your son or daughter.

■ Listen to the teacher with an open mind and try to leave preconceptions or neighborhood "rumors" about teachers out of your assessment. Remember that teachers want your child to be successful in their classes and want you to work with them to make this happen.

You will probably visit more than one teacher during the evening. Even in the elementary grades, supplemental teachers for subjects such as reading, gym, art, or music are also available to meet and greet parents. In the high school setting, you will spend a limited amount of time in the classroom of *every* teacher on your child's schedule. Depending on your individual child's needs, you may also want to introduce yourself to other professionals in the building, including the school nurse, school psychologist or child study team leader, guidance counselor, social worker, reading specialist, speech pathologist, or even the sports coach. The sheet provided below, which incorporates many of the above suggestions, can be copied and brought with you to help keep track of all of the information you receive.

Back-to-School Night
Notes and Information

CLASS NAME/NUMBER _____

TEACHER NAME _____

PHONE NUMBER _____

E-MAIL ADDRESS _____

WEB SITE INFORMATION _____

EXTRA HELP HOURS _____

Back-to-School Night
Notes and Information (cont.)

ASSESSMENT/GRADING POLICY _____

_____

_____

HOMEWORK POLICY _____

_____

_____

_____

PARENT/TEACHER CONFERENCE INFORMATION _____

OTHER INFORMATION _____

_____

_____

AFTER BACK-TO-SCHOOL NIGHT

Your school visitation evening may be over, but you will need to follow through at home in order to maximize the experience. Your child will most likely be tired or asleep when you return, so you should plan to set aside time the following day to discuss with him or her your impressions of the evening.

Since Back-to-School Night comes early in the year, it is a perfect opportunity to get the new school session off to a good start. Your reaction can influence your child's attitude, confidence, and performance for the remainder of the year. Remember to be positive about each and every teacher you met during the previous evening. Validating a student's complaints ("I know why you don't like Mr. X." or "I found Mrs. Y to be confusing, too.") will serve no purpose other than to give your child a reason not to succeed in a given class. Instead, if you find it difficult to compliment the teacher, simply acknowledge meeting him or her and discuss the information you received. You can also make a social comment such as, "I see Johnny is in your class this year" or "Maria's mom was there last night, too." Use your note sheet to review the homework policy and grading policy with your child. This will be an excellent time to review your child's schoolbooks with him or her. Also discuss what will be learned in the coming year, and review the teacher's expectations. Take this opportunity to reinforce your son's or daughter's ability to master the content and show enthusiasm about the subject material. ("Oh, I really enjoyed learning about the Civil War when I was your age." or "Wait until you see how much you are going to love this Shakespeare play!")

Now is the time to inquire about your child's notebook; ask to see his or her notes so that you can determine if he or she is organized or needs further instruction in this important study skill. Additionally, ask about pending projects and see if help from you is needed in any way. ("I heard about your forthcoming Civil War project. Do you have all of the books you need for research?" "I see you have to have this novel finished by next week. Do you want to talk about it with me?")

The point of this discussion is to let your child know that you are a partner in his or her education. Your child needs to know that you will be communicating with the school in a variety of ways, and that you are aware of the classroom workings. You can also inform your child that you will be scheduling a one-on-one meeting with the teacher to discuss specifics as related to him or her.

Your review of your Back-to-School evening is meant to remove any roadblocks to your student's success; if necessary, you need to put a positive spin on any complaints or issues your child is experiencing. Listen carefully, and if you can't solve the situation, you now have many school resource individuals who should be able to help you or give you proper direction. Do not be afraid or embarrassed to call these school professionals for help. The sooner in the year this occurs, the smoother a road your student will have as the year progresses.

CHAPTER
5

TALKING ABOUT HOMEWORK

To learn, you have to listen. To improve, you have to try.
—Thomas Jefferson

Homework. The very word makes even the best of students cringe and can cause less enthusiastic students to truly dread school altogether. Issues about homework can create stress and misery throughout a household and can even derail the educational process completely. Homework, after all, infers "work," and human nature prefers leisure to effort. It is much more fun to go out with friends, play sports, surf the Internet, or do any one of a thousand things offered outside of school.

On the other hand, good homework habits can reinforce the learning process and teach students responsibility, accountability, organizational skills, and self-management. Furthermore, homework offers parents another opportunity to support and enhance what is happening at school. If correct homework "messages" are delivered in a child's early school years, the hassles and negativity about this necessary chore can often be eliminated as the child progresses through school.

Yet there seems to be considerable confusion about the homework process itself, and parents want and need answers to their many homework-related questions. Specifically, parents wonder how little or how much help to give youngsters, how much home-

work is appropriate for students of different ages, and how homework complements a school curriculum, if at all.

UNDERSTANDING MULTIPLE INTELLIGENCES

Before answering these homework questions, it will be helpful
to understand the impact new theories of teaching and learning
have on the way students are currently being taught in classrooms
throughout the United States. In Chapter Three you read about
learning styles. The idea that individuals have specific learning styles
is derived mainly from the work of the Harvard psychologist
Howard Gardner who, in 1985, published a book titled, *Frames of
Mind: The Theory of Multiple Intelligences.* Before Gardner's research,
the majority of researchers and educators assumed that people had
a single kind of intelligence often referred to as one's IQ (Intelligence
Quotient). The popular belief was that some people were "smarter"
than others as evidenced by a higher IQ. The theory held that intelligence was a single inherited entity and that students should all be
educated in the same way with information presented in an appropriate manner.

In his seminal work, Gardner identified seven "intelligences,"
or ways individuals have of understanding information: linguistic
intelligence, logical-mathematical intelligence, musical intelligence,
bodily-kinesthetic intelligence, spatial intelligence, interpersonal
intelligence, and intrapersonal intelligence. Linguistic intelligence is
the ability to learn and use languages, and the ability to express oneself in an oral or written fashion. Writers, poets, translators, and
public speakers might be examples of people with highly developed
linguistic intelligence. Logical-mathematical intelligence manifests
itself as the ability to think logically, deduce mathematically, analyze mathematical or scientific problems, and manipulate numbers.
Obviously, mathematicians, scientists, accountants, and others in
similar fields have this type of intelligence. A person with musical
intelligence could write, perform, sing, or otherwise demonstrate

proficiency with musical patterns, rhythms, tones, and/or pitches. Musicians, conductors, lyricists, and singers display this type of intelligence. Bodily-kinesthetic intelligence is evident in a person who uses his or her body to understand the world and who solves problems using physical motion as well as mental capacity. Dancers, acrobats, gymnasts, and athletes have highly developed bodily-kinesthetic intelligences. A person with spatial intelligence can understand how things relate to one another with reference to location; this person could "see" the interrelatedness of things to given spaces. Architects, builders, and numerous workers in the trade professions possess this type of intelligence development. Gardner considered the interpersonal intelligence and the intrapersonal intelligence together: These intelligences involve the ability to understand and empathize with others and the ability to be self-reflective and understand one's own motivations and feelings. Educators, counselors, religious leaders, politicians, and different types of therapists need to have these developed intelligences.

It is important to understand that Gardner never claimed that people have only one of these types of intelligences. Rather, he asserted that individuals have unique combinations of several of these intelligences and the capacity to develop strengths in more than one area.

Traditionally, education valued only two of the seven intelligences: the linguistic and the logical-mathematical. Curriculum was designed to focus mainly on reading, writing, and arithmetic. Children who were gifted in other areas were often unable to demonstrate understanding or achieve success by using their other intelligences. These realms were designated for "outside of school."

Gardner's theories resounded with educators in North America because his theories validated what teachers witnessed daily in their classrooms. A youngster who struggled with mathematics might be able to write brilliant poems, and a student who could not understand word problems might easily manipulate geometrical shapes. One student who could not perform during physical education class demonstrated the ability to play an instrument or sing in a choir, and another who could not read well displayed understanding of a work of literature by creating a dance that reflected a specific theme.

Educators, looking for ways to connect with students who did not learn in traditional ways, now discovered new strategies to achieve this goal. Teachers and schools have reexamined whole curriculum and reinvented a number of teaching strategies and teaching models to design classrooms that reflect a new understanding about teaching and learning. Today's teachers know that students think and learn in a variety of ways, and they acknowledge that students can demonstrate real understanding using multiple types of assessments. For example, suppose a high school student has been studying the Civil War. Traditionally, the final assessment for understanding the unit might have been a single multiple-choice or essay test wherein students would have to demonstrate their understanding of the unit's content. In today's classroom, one is more likely to find multiple assessments that give students the ability to demonstrate understanding in a number of ways. One student might write a "Civil War Journal" assuming the persona of a soldier, some might compose a skit or even a song about a famous battle during the war, others might design a display of weaponry, while still another might elect to do an analysis of northern and southern war strategies.

EXPLORING BLOOM'S TAXONOMY

In addition to Howard Gardner's theories of multiple intelligences, educators today are aware of *Bloom's Taxonomy*, a system for categorizing questions that appear in educational settings. Although Benjamin Bloom's *Taxonomy of Educational Objectives: The Classification of Educational Goals: Handbook I, Cognitive Domain* was published in 1956, educators continue to find his classifications helpful. Bloom's system basically determines the level of understanding of a given topic by the skills a student can demonstrate. Bloom's Taxonomy is shown below:

COMPETENCE	Skills Demonstrated
Knowledge	■ observation and recall of information ■ knowledge of dates, events, places ■ knowledge of major ideas ■ mastery of subject matter ■ question cues: *list, define, tell, describe, identify, show, label, collect, examine, tabulate, quote, name, who, when, where*
Comprehension	■ understanding information ■ grasp meaning ■ translate knowledge into new context ■ interpret facts, compare, contrast ■ order, group, infer causes ■ predict consequences ■ question cues: *summarize, describe, interpret, contrast, predict, associate, distinguish, estimate, differentiate, discuss, extend*
Application	■ use information ■ use methods, concepts, theories in new situations ■ solve problems using required skills or knowledge ■ questions cues: *apply, demonstrate, calculate, complete, illustrate, show, solve, examine, modify, relate, change, classify, experiment, discover*

Analysis	■ seeing patterns
	■ organization of parts
	■ recognition of hidden meanings
	■ identification of components
	■ question cues:
	  analyze, separate, order, explain, connect,
	  classify, arrange, divide, compare, select,
	  explain, infer

Synthesis	■ use old ideas to create new ones
	■ generalize from given facts
	■ relate knowledge from several areas
	■ predict, draw conclusions
	■ question cues:
	  combine, integrate, modify, rearrange,
	  substitute, plan, create, design, invent,
	  compose, formulate, prepare, generalize,
	  rewrite, what if?

Evaluation	■ compare and discriminate between ideas
	■ assess value of theories, presentations
	■ make choices based on reasoned argument
	■ verify value of evidence
	■ recognize subjectivity
	■ question cues:
	  assess, decide, rank, grade, test, measure,
	  recommend, convince, select, judge,
	  explain, discriminate, support, conclude,
	  compare, summarize

Adapted from: Bloom, B.S. (Ed.) (1956) *Taxonomy of educational objectives: The classification of educational goals: Handbook I, cognitive domain.* New York; Toronto: Longmans, Green. (taken from Web site: *www.coun.uvic.ca/learn/program/hndouts/bloom.html*)

Knowledgeable educators strive to give students a deep understanding of discipline materials rather than trying to "cover" the curriculum by offering broad instruction and then calling for rote memorization. On Bloom's taxonomy, the higher-level critical-thinking skills are demonstrated by application, analysis, synthesis, and evaluation. When students transfer knowledge from one discipline to another or apply knowledge in new and creative ways, it indicates that they have indeed grasped critical concepts and have truly learned the material. A truly remarkable educational system would involve lessons and activities that taught concepts using the theories of multiple intelligences. Students would be required to use multiple skills as delineated in Bloom's Taxonomy in order to demonstrate understanding.

STUDENT-DIRECTED LEARNING

In the past, almost all classrooms focused on knowledge going in one direction: from teacher to student. Students were given information and worked individually to complete assignments for teacher review. On occasion, the entire class would be called upon to work as one, often brainstorming answers that the teacher would write on the board. Today's classrooms have moved away from this strictly one-to-one model to encompass other types of activities. Students often work in pairs or in small groups on cooperative and collaborative types of learning tasks. Teachers understand that in the real world most students will be involved in jobs that involve some level of teamwork. Training students to work effectively in groups prepares them for success in future endeavors. Group work teaches students how to set common goals, how to divide tasks fairly among group members, how to negotiate disagreements between group members, and how to achieve consensus. Students working effectively in small groups can support and encourage one another and learn a great deal from the exchange of information and collaboration among group members.

THE HOMEWORK CONNECTION

How does all of this effect a given homework assignment? Knowing what is happening in your child's classroom is imperative to being effective at reinforcing the work done at home. Understanding the goals of teachers and the skills that are valued in the classroom can give you perspective on the assignments your child is given to complete independently.

Teachers use homework to help students review, practice, or extend work that was done in the classroom or to assess understanding of given concepts that have previously been taught. Homework is also used as a way for students to explore topics and research ideas that have been initially presented in a classroom setting. You can see how Bloom's Taxonomy, works with homework, which is often an opportunity for students to apply information or demonstrate deep understanding of concepts in a specific discipline. Homework that is meaningful and that reinforces work done in school can be instrumental toward obtaining real knowledge. However, homework should not be done in a vacuum; the teacher should be reading it and offering constructive criticism and praise on completed assignments. Parents can also share in this feedback process.

Too often, homework is a mystery to parents. They don't know what homework was given, why it was given, when it is due, or how they are supposed to help in the process. For homework to be of value to students, it should be meaningful, have clear, concise directions, and be aligned with a student's ability level and knowledge base. Furthermore, it is helpful if homework offers choices that appeal to a variety of multiple intelligences or learning styles.

Most teachers will explain their homework policy on Back-to-School Night. (See Chapter 4.) Teachers' expectations about the homework process may vary. Some will want you to monitor a child's homework or extend help as needed. Others will want parents to simply check that it has been done or to check for certain types of errors. No matter the extent of your involvement with your child's homework, it ultimately provides the opportunity for a partnership that promotes successful habits of mind and contributes to increased academic excellence.

Elementary and Middle School Students

For children in elementary school, homework is one of the first opportunities for them to feel like "grown-up" students. It is also the first step toward their becoming independent learners and thinkers. This is the time to begin to set homework parameters that will remain in place as your child ascends the academic ladder. The early elementary grades are the time for students to develop habits and attitudes that will support them later in life. Middle school students will need to begin more independent activities that can prepare them for high school learning. What follows are some guidelines specifically designed for beginning and middle school learners:

Have a Positive Outlook

Homework is meant to be a positive experience. Homework must never be viewed by children as a form of punishment or a vehicle for severe criticism or fighting with parents. If a child is having chronic homework problems, you need to examine the issues involved. If your child fails to complete homework on a regular basis, consistently cries that he or she can not do the work, or seems to need more help than you think is reasonable, you need to make an appointment with the teacher. Teachers can suggest certain strategies for parents to help students over this "homework hump." In certain cases, teachers might even suggest extra tutoring. Consistent homework frustrations indicate a need to develop a plan of action to forestall further impediments to education.

Designate a Study Place

Setting up a specific study place is key to your child's homework success. If possible, set up a study area that contains good lighting and a place for all of your child's study supplies. (See Chapter 3 for more tips.) Many younger students need or want to do assignments in the kitchen or at another location close to mom or dad. Students like the feeling of having you close by in case they have questions. It is important for either you or a caregiver to be nearby and serve as a resource for your child. Your child might want your help to review spelling words or to clarify something in a textbook. Helping is fine as long as you remember that it is his or her homework, not yours. You are a coach, but you cannot run the race for your child. These days, the pressures for success begin as early as the elementary grades, and sometimes, in haste to have children be "the best," parents take an overly active role in completing homework. Don't forget, one of the reasons teachers give homework is to assess your child's understanding of a particular topic. If you do the work, the teacher will not know how much your child has really understood.

Schedule Study Time

Children need to know that parents value education and the homework associated with it. If you create a *daily* time when the entire house is engaged in quiet activity, your child will have this behavior modeled for him or her. It can be a time when you do bookkeeping chores, write notes, read, or complete other similar activities. Knowing that other family members also attend to "thinking" tasks during this quiet time will go a long way toward breaking a child's resistance to homework activity. Elementary school children need help to develop a specific homework schedule. You can help him or her write one up and post it on the refrigerator door. Younger children might not have daily homework, but they should be encouraged to maintain a daily study time nonetheless. Your child can use this time for reading, writing, or other academic activity.

Turn Off the Television!

Television seems to be the universal distracter of homework. Young children are in the process of learning how to study, and it is important to provide an atmosphere that supports productive study habits. Try as they might, youngsters cannot ignore a TV program or focus on reading while hearing background television dialogue.

Monitor Assignments

Buy your child an assignment pad if the school does not provide one. Get him or her into the practice of writing down all homework or projects from school. If something is supposed to be brought to school, make sure that your child writes that down. When your child returns from school (or in the evening when you return from work), make certain to ask him or her to share the assignment pad with you. For younger children, this can happen simultaneously with emptying their book bags and giving you all required notes and notices. This will keep you informed about what is happening in school, send the message to your child that you are interested in his or her schoolwork, and help teach the organizational skills that are so important to student success. If you are not home when your child completes his or her homework, make certain to review it when you are available. Similarly, when homework is returned by the teacher, make certain to review the comments with your child so that he or she can see the final assessment.

Monitor the Length of Homework Time

Parents often ask how long homework should take for elementary students. Generally, educators believe that homework is most effective for children in grades K to 3 when it does not exceed twenty minutes every day. Twenty to forty minutes per day is usually effective for grades 4 to 6. For grades 7 and 8, students might have up to two hours of homework, since they will be taking classes in multiple disciplines. If your child struggles regularly to complete assignments within a reasonable time frame, you should make an appointment to speak with his or her teacher. Your child may be distracted by things happening in the household, or it may be that there are other issues that need addressing. Similarly, if your child is finishing the homework assignments too quickly, encourage him or her to look over the work carefully or to read additional materials to reinforce the lesson. Remember that study breaks are a key element in the homework process. Students, especially younger ones, need frequent breaks in order to recharge and refocus on their work. Naturally, if a child is focused and enjoying an assignment, then wait until he or she seems to need a few minutes of relaxation before suggesting a break. If desired, use the Homework Log at the end of this chapter to keep track of work completed.

Schedule Work for Long-Term Assignments

You will want to invest in a large monthly calendar, or you might print one from the computer. Encourage your son or daughter to write down long-term assignments or test dates so that he or she learns to do a bit at a time and not procrastinate on assignments. Seeing posted assignments allows you to offer gentle reminders about due dates and necessary studying and helps students remember what is due and when it is due. Long-term assignments can be overwhelming because they require a great deal of advance preparation—often on the part of the parent as well as the student! It is important to help students break down these large assignments into manageable "chunks" of study time. Help your younger child write out the steps necessary to complete the longer assignment, and determine how and when each portion will be completed. Your child should learn to check off each portion as he or she finishes it. He or she will apply these same skills to studying for tests.

Talk About the Assignments

Talking about assignments with students can be helpful on many different levels. Talking is a prelude to thinking and a form of prewriting; when a student talks about his or her work, a "plan of action" often forms in the mind and he or she understands how to begin the task. Talking also clarifies the subject matter and reinforces the requirements of the assignment. Finally, talking lets students know that you are interested in their work and that you are there to support them. Ask questions that will help clarify the homework task and help you to understand where your child may need help. Read the directions on the assignment and ask your son or daughter to paraphrase them for you to see if the meaning is properly understood. Making sure that at the outset directions are understood will go a long way to preventing later frustration or anger. It is often helpful to use a highlighter to clarify and remind students about the specifics in a set of directions. For example, if a writing prompt asks about the characters in a book, make certain to underline the *s* so that students remember to choose more than one character. If an assignment uses words like *list, compare, describe,* or *define,* students should get in the habit of highlighting these types of words. Key words in math problems should also be highlighted so that students know exactly what is required of them. Sometimes a student will need to articulate the steps of a given assignment to clearly understand them and develop a homework plan.

Motivate with Praise

Praise builds self-confidence and gives students a reason to continue to perform to the best of their abilities. Younger children, in particular, strive to please parents and respond positively to parental encouragement. "Good job!" goes a long way toward reinforcing behavior and attitudes that you want repeated. If a child has not performed well on a given task, you need to discover why. Calm questions such as, "Did you understand the directions?" or "Do you need me to help you with that?" can defuse anger or frustration that will result in negative feelings. Make certain that your child knows the high expectations you have for his or her work, and praise the effort it takes to reach those expectations. When especially good homework is returned, younger children love to see it displayed on the refrigerator or elsewhere for all to see. Provide folders for completed homework so that your child knows that work should arrive at school without rips, tears, or folds. Again, if a child knows that you value his or her efforts, he or she will be more apt to repeat the performance. Do not be afraid to provide constructive criticism when needed; just be aware of phrasing it in a way that does not negate the child's entire effort. Find something positive to say about the assignment and then let him or her know how or where it might be improved. ("I love the story you have written...do you think you want to copy it onto lined paper?")

Don't Go Overboard

Provide the help and support your child needs without doing the work yourself. There is nothing more frustrating for a teaching professional than assigning homework and getting back work that is obviously not the student's own. If you understand the reasons for homework (as outlined above) then you will know when to provide help and when to let your child work alone. Essentially, if you provide the place to do homework, the quiet time in which to study, the supplies needed, and the review of the task to be accomplished, your child should be given the opportunity to show what he or she understands and is able to do. When the assignment is complete, you can read, review, praise, and practice when appropriate. Give children the time and space to work through what they are learning—and, importantly, give them ownership of their own work. There is nothing that feels better than struggling and finally mastering a given concept or problem. Let your child learn to feel the pride in accomplishing this mastery on his or her own, and let the inevitable mistakes along the way become lessons. Clearly, if a child has homework issues night after night, it is a sign that a teacher conference is in order to see if you both can solve the problems at hand. Likewise, if a child has an upcoming test, help him or her review the material. You can be a coach, but you should never play in the game. If a child needs help with a problem or an explanation of a project, go ahead and offer your help. If it is not something you understand, suggest that he or she mark the problem and ask the teacher about it the next day. Always remember that it is your child's homework, not yours.

Identify Your Child's Learning Style

Homework efforts can be enhanced by knowing your child's preferred learning style. Earlier in this chapter and in Chapter 3, the idea of learning styles was reviewed. If you understand how your child learns best, you can reinforce concepts and information learned in school. This is particularly important with younger students who may need review with basic concepts in arithmetic or language arts. For example, if your child is a visual learner, you might use pictures, charts, or graphs to demonstrate vocabulary, spelling, or math concepts taught at school. If your child's best learning style is auditory, it may help if you repeat certain things aloud while he or she listens. Similarly, if a child is a kinesthetic learner, it can help if he or she can use manipulatives to reinforce a given lesson.

 ## *High School Students*

High school students present a whole other dimension of the homework process. By the time students are in high school, they feel independent and do not want mom or dad looking over their shoulders or reexamining their homework. In addition, there are many more distractions to accomplishing homework including after-school activities, social engagements, part-time jobs, sports activities, computer games and instant messaging, and, of course, television. It is also a given that older students will have more homework than younger ones. It is assumed that their organizational skills, as well as their ability to concentrate, are further developed and therefore high school students should be capable of longer, more involved assignments. If good study habits were begun early enough, your son or daughter may well have assimilated them into their daily academic routine. If these good habits are not well entrenched as yet, all is not lost. The good news is that, although it may take more effort to guide older students to demonstrate good study habits, it is really never too late to learn this skill. Parents of high school students will certainly hear complaining and receive resistance if this is the first time that they have made these types of demands on their children. However, with calm but firm resolve, homework can become less work for the entire household.

All of the homework tips outlined in the earlier section for younger students also apply, at least to some degree, for the high school student. Parents can be in the background subtly overseeing the implementation of these parameters. Students should find a comfortable, quiet place to study that is relatively free from household distractions. Students at this age should have moved away from the kitchen table or other center of family activity to a place they can concentrate better. Sometimes, students of this age will want to study on their beds, with the door to their room closed and the music blasting. The bed is not the best place to study as the lighting is usually not adequate, and students of this age may opt for a quick nap over studying. A desk or table works much better; the surface should be large enough to spread out all materials, and hold a computer, if one is available. Some students find that music helps them to concentrate; if this is your son or daughter's learning style, that may well be true. The most important thing is that the music does not distract them from focusing on their studies.

Many times, when parents of high school students ask about their homework, students will reply, "I don't have any," or "I did it in school." Additionally, parents of high school students are often not home after school and cannot oversee the start of the homework process. High school students need a study plan even more so than younger students. They must consider how much homework they have for a given night and balance that against sports or other activity commitments for that day. Here are some specific suggestions geared to students in grades 9-12.

Help Organize a Study Space

Organize a study space with your child at the beginning of the year and insist that he or she keep it as clean and clutter-free as possible. Help your child set up files for individual subjects and keep one folder for transporting completed assignments to and from school. There is nothing worse than taking care to do an assignment and then having it rip or get lost at home or in a bookbag. Ensure that reference books such as dictionaries or a thesaurus are close at hand, that a computer or other word processing equipment is on the desk, and that pencils, pens, highlighters, paper clips, scissors, and a stapler are nearby. Make certain that the study chair is comfortable; it should support your son's or daughter's back and be the correct height for the desk or table. Providing a bulletin board on which to "tack up" important information and a large-spaced calendar will also help your student with long-term planning.

Plan for Homework and Study Time

This may sound obvious, but planning is probably the most important thing one can do to maximize the study session. The first step must start in school. Students must write down every assignment in their organizer or notebook when the teacher gives the homework. It is virtually impossible to remember the homework assignments in all subject areas at the end of a day. A student should be proactive by asking the teacher questions about home-work at the time it is given. Students need to completely understand an assignment in order to do well. It is easier to take a moment and clarify a question than to spend hours at night trying to find an answer to a particular question. A student might even ask a teacher how long a specific assignment should take so that he or she can better budget their time on task. Long-term assignments will be frequent in the high school setting. It is imperative that your child divide these tasks in chunks and do some each night until the job is complete. A student cannot do an exceptional job in one night if the task was meant to be done over several weeks or months. Writing out the assignment and then designating exactly which steps will be done when is the only way to ensure that the long-term task is completed correctly without last minute panic or frustration. A student in high school should also devote nightly time to academic work whether or not he or she has a specific assignment. There is always reading to be done, notes to be reviewed or rewritten, or tests that one can study for in advance. Parents who enforce this mandatory study time will find that students will read more, study harder, and most likely do better in classes.

Encourage Use of Study Hall Time

Many high schools schedule a study hall period into a student's day. This is usually a quiet, supervised time when students can work on studying or assignments. High school homework does take a sizeable chunk out of every evening; if a student can complete one or two tasks during a study hall period, it will lessen the evening's work load. For some students a study hall is too distracting for actual studying, but it may be a good time to read or organize the evening's work. It may be tempting for your son or daughter to socialize with friends during a free period in school, but remind them that using study hall time appropriately will free up hours later for other enjoyable tasks.

Don't Tolerate Procrastination

Using time beneficially is what time management is all about. After laying out a plan of study, it is important to get right to work. If a student is at his or her desk or study area, he or she should be able to focus and get right to work. One useful hint is to begin with the most difficult assignments and leave the easier tasks for last. It may be enticing to get the easier things finished first, but one is usually most focused at the beginning of the task, so it is best to use this time on the things that take the most concentration. Many students find that if they check off the completed assignment on an assignment list, they can see their progress and derive a sense of accomplishment by finishing the task.

Get Help When Necessary

Remember that homework is an assessment of how well one has understood the subject material or grasped a particular concept. If a student has difficulties that are not clarified by the teacher, that student must consider taking other steps to get help as soon as possible. If too much time passes, a student will get further and further behind and begin to hate a particular class or feel that it is too hard. Remember that every student has his or her own learning style, and sometimes learning a concept in a different way is all that it will take to succeed. There are multiple options for help in a given subject area. If one's teacher is unavailable or unable to help, perhaps another teacher in that same discipline can be of assistance. Sometimes, schools provide expert tutors; these can be either students who are adept in a given area or adult volunteers. If necessary, you can call a department head, a guidance counselor, or a school principal and get the names of professional tutors who help students. These tutors are paid for their services, but it may be that your child simply needs a few extra, focused hours in order to better understand the subject matter. For longer periods of help, consider the numerous tutoring centers that have recently opened around the country. These centers, which work with students after school hours, help in specific content areas, or help students become more proficient with general study skills.

Set Clear Expectations

Do not be afraid to let your son or daughter know what you expect. Remember that high school students only have four years in which to prepare themselves for the independent work ethic that college will demand. Nightly homework assignments teach the skills that students will need to implement on their own when they are away from home. Parents of high school students still need to show interest, discuss assignments and readings, and offer praise to encourage good study habits. Discussion about assignments are warm-ups for the task, no different than the athletic warm-up before a race or big game. When a student discusses a completed assignment, he or she reinforces concepts learned by explanation and repetition. Involved parents are often amazed at the depth of their child's understanding of a particular content area; often students are learning subjects that parents never encountered at school. Rather than feeling inadequate, parents can ask students to "teach" them the materials; remember, teaching is one of the highest categories of critical thinking on Bloom's Taxonomy. Students and parents sharing lessons become a small learning community, and lifelong learning and knowledge acquisition is modeled for the student.

Keep Track of Grades

Encourage your son or daughter to keep track of his or her grades. Many times a student will not understand why he or she received a certain grade on a report card. Usually, it is because he or she forgot to factor in a certain quiz or missing homework assignment. There will be far less anger, frustration, and surprise if you encourage the habit of recording graded papers as soon as they are returned. With the advent of electronic grade book programs, teachers often periodically print out a student's grades at different points in the marking period. These can be kept in a specific folder to alleviate questions about the assessment process. If a grade is not understood, it is important to schedule a conference with the teacher to discuss the discrepancy.

The forms that follow can be adapted for learners in grades K through 12 and will serve to organize students and help with management of their assignments.

LONG-TERM ASSIGNMENT PLANNER

Use this sheet to break down long-term assignments into smaller tasks. Use a calendar and record the due dates for each section of the assignment. For every step, write down exactly what task you will accomplish. (For example: get library book, take notes, interview person X, write rough draft.)

Assignment: _____   **Due Date:** _____

Step One: _____   **Due Date:** _____

Step Two: _____   **Due Date:** _____

Step Three: _____   **Due Date:** _____

Step Four: _____   **Due Date:** _____

Step Five: Proofread rough draft and have someone look over the assignment   **Due Date:** _____

(One week BEFORE assignment due date)

HOMEWORK LOG		
Assignment Due Date	Assigned Task	Date Completed

ASSESSMENT LOG

Record grades for every assignment returned to keep track of marking period progress.

Date Returned	Assignment	Grade Received

CHAPTER

6

READING THE NEWSPAPER

Were it left to me to decide whether we should have a government without newspapers, or newspapers without a government, I should not hesitate a moment to prefer the latter.
—*Thomas Jefferson, 1787*

The history of the United States of America is virtually inseparable from the history of its journalism. Newspapers, from the very beginning of our country's history, have provided our democratic society with the information upon which we can make informed decisions, both politically and socially. Originally, clumsy, one-sheet flyers were created by hand or by setting the type letter by letter. These soon developed into longer, more informative newspapers created on still-clumsy printing presses; however, as technological expertise raced ahead, so, too, did the newspaper industry. Newspapers eventually became a burgeoning business in our country, and they became indispensable for citizens wanting to remain knowledgeable. The information explosion, which today is associated with the widespread accessibility of the television and the computer, all began with newspapers.

Not many years ago, a great majority of families subscribed to one or two daily papers (often morning and evening editions) and spent hours reading every section of the paper. The newspaper, for many, was the sole source of news and information, and provided a forum for reading and voicing public opinion. Today, although this form of mass media still wields an enormous influence over life in this country, it is apparent that the younger generation does not have the same affinity for newspapers as their parents did. In fact, newspapers are losing subscribers, as more and more news is accessed through the computer. A "flash" headline delivered in print cannot compete with breaking news delivered immediately over the Internet. Journalistic survival has meant learning to adapt to this shift, and newspapers now tend to concentrate on other perspectives of a story rather than attempting to be the first with newsbreaking headline stories.

Every parent and educator is aware that even our youngest children are bombarded with an uncountable array of media on a daily basis. Television, radio, the Internet, billboard advertising, print ads, CDs, DVDs, and big screen movies have invaded our way of life as never before. Whereas years ago parents were mainly concerned about the effect of television commercials on young children, today parental concerns about media influence are far greater. Images and ads that stream across the Internet reach children as never before. Children are inundated with media messages, and studies have suggested that some children spend as much time in front of a TV or computer screen as they do playing outside. As students get older, they are subjected to more and more media messages, many of which are geared toward the vulnerable and the uneducated. Students need the tools and skills to help them interpret the media messages that come into their lives. We want students to learn how to discern the valuable messages from the invaluable ones, to become critical consumers and educated and worldly civilians. In order to succeed in the new millenium, students need to be media-literate. They must learn how to read, interpret, analyze, understand, and evaluate the media thrust upon them on a daily basis. Students have to be taught how to make sense of the news and how to decide if it is credible. Teaching media literacy is teaching students to think critically about the world around them.

Most states now have a component of media literacy reflected in their states' educational standards. Young people tend to use media for entertainment and not for education. After all, entertainment is fun and takes far less effort. Youngsters who are used to screen media (television, computers, movies) may be less inclined to put forth the effort required to read a newspaper on a daily basis.

So, why should you encourage your child from a very early age to learn to read the newspaper? Newspapers do more than just deliver the news to the public; they can begin your child's journey into media-literacy. Reading the newspaper can begin a student's awareness of one type of media and can serve to enhance basic skills in every possible subject area. Newspapers teach reading, math, science, social studies, language arts, art, statistics, economics, and every other subject. Furthermore, the newspaper is an inexpensive teaching tool that can be used for any age student, at any ability level. Unlike textbooks, the newspaper is a living document that changes daily and that presents students with unlimited information and learning opportunities.

Preschool and Elementary Students

As discussed in other chapters of this book, a parent is a child's first teacher. You should encourage your preschool and elementary student to "read" the newspaper with you. Reading can be a special time for you both to share your thoughts and interests as well as for you to encourage an appreciation of words and reading. There are hundreds of activities for every age student on almost every page of any daily newspaper. Outlined here are a number of activities particularly appropriate for preschool and elementary students, followed by ways that middle school and high school students might use the daily paper. At the end of this chapter you will find newspaper activities delineated by subject area, so if you and your child want specific practice in a given content area, you might use some of the suggestions from this list. Remember that any of the activities can be adjusted for a wide variety of children's ability levels and interests. As you use these suggestions to encourage newspaper use, you will likely find yourself discovering your own original activities that you and your child can share!

The Letter Search Game

Invite young children to search through the newspaper for all the different letters of the alphabet. Have children find capital letters, small letters, letters in different fonts, and letters in different colors. Once they can identify the letters, preschoolers can work to cut out the letters with blunt nose (kindergarten or safety) scissors. Children can either make a letter poster or you can help them create an ABC book. Each page might contain all the different *A*s or *B*s or *C*s the child discovered in the paper. Next, children might even locate newspaper pictures that start with each of the discovered letters.

A Mystery Scavenger Hunt

After reading the paper, give your child a list of things he must find as he looks through the first few pages (or just the front page) of the paper. Perhaps he might search for a number, a policeman, a picture of a car, a capital letter *A*. Adjust the hunt based on the ability level of the child. Children love playing the newspaper hunt game.

Sharing Interesting Articles

Reading and then talking about short, appropriate articles will help children learn the structure of informational writings and will serve to broaden their vocabulary and general knowledge. Reading aloud to children will also serve to lengthen their attention span, teach them to listen for details, and begin to teach listening and visualization skills.

Fun with Comic Strips

Most children, through television, are aware of the nature of a cartoon. Show your child the comic pages and explain how comics are similar to cartoons. Point out that comic strips also have characters who "say" things to one another; explain that the bubbles indicate what the characters are saying.

Exploring Newspaper Format

Elementary students are not too young to understand the distinction between headlines and articles. Point out to them that news headlines are like book titles. (They announce what the article is going to be about.) Children can start by pointing out the headlines from the articles. They can even cut out and create two different piles, one for the headlines and one for the articles. Show your child the different sections of the newspaper and explain the purpose of the sports pages, the national and local news, and the classified pages. Demonstrate how ads look different from the articles and discuss the purposes of each. Articles give us information while ads are intended to influence us to make a purchase.

Creating a Hero File

Help students create a file or scrapbook with articles on policemen, firefighters, and other heroes they might identify. Speak about the job and what the person actually does on a daily basis. You can follow up on any specific interests by taking your youngster to the firehouse, the police station, or on other suitable outings.

Teaching About Sequence

Cut apart a comic strip into separate frames and then have your child put it back together. Discuss what happens first, second, and third. This helps children learn sequence and logical order.

Writing Your Own Comic Strip

Have young students make up a story. Ask them to draw the pictures of the story into frames like those in the comic strips. Help them to write the words in the comic "bubbles." This activity begins instruction in elementary dialogue and practices sequence and transitions ("first this happened, then this, then this . . .") for young writers.

Following an Ongoing News Story

Help children follow an ongoing story over several days. Remind them of what happened on the previous day and have them recount the additional information they learn on subsequent days. This will give children an excellent insight into the way that news is reported in the paper and the way that information is updated on a daily basis. Save all of the stories about a particular event so that your child can make a small "book" about that news story.

Using Grocery Ads

Use grocery ads so that your child can help with the weekly shopping list. Children can find pictures of foods you specify and cut them out to create a personalized shopping list. When you go to the store, youngsters can bring their list and match their pictures with the actual foods purchased. Elementary students can also use the grocery lists to practice planning healthy, well-balanced meals.

Creating a Scrapbook

Children can look through the paper and collect articles and pictures about a particular interest or hobby they may have. Sports, pets, flowers, or science articles can be collected over a period of time and students can create an "interest scrapbook" on that particular topic. Encourage them to share their interest book with other children or other adults in the household.

Reinforcing Positive Social Values

As you read through the paper, highlight stories you can share with youngsters about positive role models. Seek out stories about people who have made good choices, people who have helped others, or about other exemplary citizens. Use these articles to discuss these situations and to help children understand the values encouraged in our society.

Middle School Students

Middle school students have a better understanding of the news and its relationship to local, national, and international events. They can also better understand the multiple jobs (editor, reporter, printer, advertiser, photographer) associated with a newspaper and the process involved in moving from the created word to the actual daily paper. Using the newspaper with middle school students serves to broaden their understanding of the world and teach them important concepts related to current events. It can also enrich their knowledge in every field studied in school, including history, geography, reading, literature, math, science, media literacy, art, music, and almost anything else you can name. The activities listed below are particularly appropriate for the middle school student.

Mapping the News

Use local, national, and international news to enhance your child's understanding of geography. A good way to do this is to get a globe or world map and identify the locale of particularly interesting news stories. Identifying the location of the story will make the story come alive for the youngster. If your child does not know much about the city or country featured in the piece, use this opportunity to do a mini research assignment about it. A broad overview of the locale can easily be found via the Internet or in a general encyclopedia.

Scanning for Information

Make up a list of "Twenty Questions" about various articles, using one or more sections of the paper depending on the age or ability level of the student. Ask your child to try to find out the answers. This will require him or her to scan the headlines and articles and then to locate appropriate answers. This game teaches important scanning skills that are easily transferable to school situations, such as scanning a textbook for information and reading for high-stakes tests. Students can be timed and challenged to find the answers in a certain number of minutes.

Writing Your Own Newspaper

Using any number of easy-to-use software programs such as Microsoft Word or Microsoft Publisher, middle school students can plan and write their own newspaper. They can name the paper, research and write news stories, draw or import artwork, do interviews, or write book and restaurant reviews. The news stories can focus on simple things like family events: a wedding, new job, new home, birth of a baby, a birthday or anniversary—almost anything will work. Students can print out their completed newspapers and distribute them to family members.

Becoming a News Expert

Have middle school students identify an area of interest: a specific news story, a particular field of interest, a sports figure or national figure, or a specific trend reported in the news. Invite them to follow that interest daily, weekly, or monthly in the newspaper. Students should be encouraged to clip out the information on their topic, and to organize a file or scrapbook so that they can follow it from the beginning. This activity reinforces organizational skills, summarizing skills, and reading skills, and allows students to feel like a resident expert in a particular subject. After a few weeks, the students will be able to speak knowledgably on a specific topic that has been tracked in the newspaper.

Writing Headlines

Headlines are usually phrases that summarize the focus of a given article. Start this "game" by having students match a stack of news articles to their corresponding headlines, which are gathered at random in another stack. Students will gain practice by reading the articles and trying to identify their main ideas. Once students become adept at this matching game, it is time to have them try to write their own headlines. Cut out specific articles and have students try to create their own headlines. Students will not only practice the important skill of concise writing, but will learn how to state the main idea in a succinct manner. Make sure to praise all efforts, especially the more creative ones!

News Versus Feature Articles

Discuss the obvious differences between news and feature articles, and determine the purpose of each. Read a few examples of each type of article with your child and explain how to identify the traits of each type of writing. Work with him or her to find the "5 Ws" in the news story. Who? What? Where? Why? When? Your child might even use a highlighter to locate and underline the factual answers to these questions. Students can practice writing a news article for an upcoming event and then write a feature article on the same topic. For example, using the 5 Ws, your child might write a news article about an upcoming test in social studies. After the test, he might try to write a feature article about "test taking" or "how to conquer test-taking nervousness." Manipulating stories in this way will give exceptionally good practice for writing with a specific sense of purpose, audience, tone, and voice.

Adding to Ads

Have your child identify particularly effective ads. Discuss why that ad is so appealing. It may be the graphics, the language, or a combination of a number of factors that makes it attractive. Have your child highlight the item that is advertised, and then highlight all of the adjectives used to describe that item. Work with your child to create new adjectives (funnier ones, sadder ones, crazier ones) to describe the same item. Not only does this stimulate a child's manipulation of grammar, but it is an excellent way to increase vocabulary! Children love to draw, so encourage your child to draw his or her own ads using new words and original pictures. You will be amazed at the creative results of this fun game.

Practicing Math

Middle school students can use newspaper ads to reinforce math concepts taught at school. Students can add, subtract, multiply, and divide to keep track of grocery savings, to "purchase" multiple items, and to total goods on a shopping list. You can also create mini word problems using the information found in almost any newspaper ad and have your youngster work through those problems with you.

Reading Reviews

Show middle school students how to read reviews of movies or television shows. Students can read reviews and then compare them with their own perceptions after viewing the described film or TV show. Students can also practice writing their own movie reviews by emulating a review they have read in the paper using a film they have seen for themselves.

Writing in Sequence

Organizing writing into a logical sequence is an important skill taught in school. Your middle school student can practice learning to sequence with this fun activity. Find a news story that has a clear set of specific chronological events. Cut the story into "strips" of information, with a different strip for every step in the sequence. See if your child can put the strips into the proper sequence within a set amount of time so that the story makes sense. Make sure to discuss the reasons that a specific sequence is the logically correct one to use.

Adjective or Adverb ABCs

Take any single page (or section) of the newspaper and challenge your child to find an adjective that begins with each letter of the alphabet. The list might look like this: American, beautiful, cold, dry, elegant, and so on. Continue the list until your child reaches the letter Z. Try racing with him or her to see who can find the most words in a given amount of time. This activity works equally well with adverbs, and can even be done with verbs and nouns if your child needs practice with these grammatical structures.

Creating a Crossword Puzzle or Word Search

Have your child find twenty-five interesting words from the newspaper. Encourage him or her to look up their meanings and then invite your child to create either a word search or a crossword puzzle with them. A friend, a sibling, or a parent can try to solve the original puzzle.

Rewriting Articles

Locate a small news article written in either the present or past tense. Have your child rewrite the article changing tenses. For an extra challenge, he or she might try to write the article in the future tense.

High School Students

High school students have as much to gain as their younger counterparts by reading a daily newspaper. The newspaper can enhance vocabulary that will appear on the ACT or SAT College Entrance Exams and can help students become better thinkers and more analytical writers. High school students often want to be "in the know" and may read the paper just to become conversant about issues that their peers are discussing at school. In every case, the paper can provide an important resource for supplementing school instruction and extending classroom content. High school students should be reading the paper on their own; parents should look for numerous opportunities to open family discussions that relate to specific local, national, and international events. As with many other behaviors, when high school students see that newspaper reading is modeled by their parents, it becomes an accepted part of their environment. Your child will learn that an important part of citizenship is the obligation to be well informed; if mature adults in his or her life value this mode of exchanging information, your teenager will also want to partake in reading the news. High school students should be comfortable with the following activities:

Examining News Sources

High school students should understand the differences among a wide variety of news sources: the Internet, the television, the radio, and the news print. To understand the subtle and not-so-subtle perspectives of the different media sources, students should identify a specific news story and examine the way the story is reported in each of these sources.

Working on a Newspaper

The best way to understand the newspaper is to actually work at creating one. Most high school students have the opportunity to work on their school papers, and even some middle schools have school papers. Students can choose a role that interests them—advertising, layout, writing, photography, or business management—and offer to work on the school paper in that role. Not only does this give students an excellent perspective on the way that news is made, but it is a wonderful way to experience possible career options while serving the school. Furthermore, colleges love to see high school students involved in extracurricular activities that enhance their communication skills on many fronts—and working on the school paper does just that.

The Editorial Page

High school students should become aware that the newspaper provides an exceptional forum for hearing the opinions of others and for voicing one's own opinion. First, work with your child to examine a typical newspaper editorial. Preferably, you should pick a topic about which the student is knowledgeable or concerned. (Consider topics such as the teen driving age, drug prevention, alcohol abuse, school violence, rock music, sports issues, and school budgets.) There are numerous activities that can be done with an editorial:

1. Read the editorial and help your child identify the point of view of the author. (This skill will help in English class and in many later high-stakes tests.)

2. Try to locate another editorial elsewhere on the same topic. Discuss the ways in which the editorials are similar and the ways in which they are different. Identify whether or not the points of view of the articles are similar or dissimilar and try to identify how and why this is so.

3. Find a news story on the same topic as one of the editorials. Compare the two accounts and discuss the major differences between a news story and an editorial.

4. Examine the editorial to identify the persuasive strategies and word choices used by the author to influence the reader. These strategies can be practiced and replicated in your student's own writing.

5. Finally, encourage your son or daughter to write a letter to the editor expressing a strong feeling about a specific topic. Seeing one's letter in print is an excellent way of reinforcing writing for a purpose and an important lesson on civic duty.

Comparing and Contrasting

Once again, this is an important skill that will be called upon throughout your child's schooling. Have your child locate news articles on the same topic in at least two different sources. Using one highlight color, he or she should highlight the points that appear in both articles. Using another highlighter color, he or she should indicate information that appears in only one of the sources. Discuss both articles with emphasis on each writer's particular choice about what information to include or exclude. Discuss also how those choices strengthened or weakened the authors' main arguments.

Political Cartoons

Your high school student should be made aware of the use of political cartoons to communicate controversial ideas or opinions. Students should be able to "read" the message behind the cartoons and should practice articulating the cartoonist's purpose. Students may want to take a controversial topic and attempt to create a political cartoon of their own that expresses their personal views on the subject.

Surveys, Graphs, and Charts

Newspapers have a large array of surveys, graphs, and charts that high school students should become adept at understanding. Learning how to read this type of information allows students to practice important analytical skills and teaches them how to cull information from a myriad of resources. Students who are new to this type of skill can start by graphing basic weather information over a period of days or weeks and eventually move on to more involved types of statistical analyses. Creating a bar, line, or picture graph of their own will show students how pictorial information is often more helpful than longer, written explanations.

Becoming Discerning Consumers

High school students are exposed to over 3,000 ads a day, according to one Internet source. They also buy many different material things and influence parents to buy even more. Billions of dollars of our economy originate from teenage spending. Students should be aware of the ways that advertisers target specific consumer groups such as teens, and they must learn to assess advertisements for a variety of propaganda. Examination of newspaper ads is an excellent way to become aware of the subtlety of words and word choices, and the subliminal messages sent through the use of photography.

Understanding Trends in Labor

Students in high school can use newspaper information to discern and analyze specific information. For example, a student might accumulate several weeks' worth of classified ads. Using these ads, he or she should see if there are any observable employment trends, such as several ads for a specific type of job, or possibly a lack of need in a particular field. Your child might want to note down specific job salaries, and even draw conclusions about supply and demand from that evidence. The follow-up would include searching for articles that relate to the employment trends noted.

Subject-Specific
Newspaper Activities

The activities that follow are arranged not by grade level but by subject area. Activities are adaptable to a wide variety of student ability and maturity levels. If your child needs reinforcement in a particular content area, consider using some of these activities to make practice more like a game!

MATHEMATICS ACTIVITIES

Number Search

In a given amount of time, see how many numbers from 1 to 100 can be found in the newspaper. The person who circles the most numbers in that time is the winner.

Make Up Equations

Manipulate any two numbers found on a page in the newspaper: Add the numbers, subtract the numbers, multiply and divide the numbers.

Spending Money

Using the prices on any ads, try to spend exactly $100. The person getting the most for his or her money, without going over the original amount, is the winner.

Mathematics Vocabulary

Find and cut out math words from the paper. These can be any words used in a mathematical sense: *all, less, more, none, any, fewer, equal, unequal, divide, multiply, add, subtract, annual, weekly*. Have younger students create a poster or small book with these math terms; older students might generate an ongoing vocabulary list including antonyms and synonyms for the terms.

Solving Word Problems

Write out a word problem whose answer can be found in the newspaper. Challenge your child to solve the problem by searching for the answer in the news.

Recipe Magic

Find delicious sounding recipes in the home section of the paper. (Desserts work especially well!) Students practice making the recipe for more or less people by doubling or halving the ingredients. As a reward, help your child create that actual yummy dish.

Learning About Percents

When children first learn about percentages, it is helpful for them to relate that knowledge to authentic information. Students can find uses for percents or can even use a ruler to figure out what percent of a page of paper is taken up by ads or pictures.

LANGUAGE ARTS ACTIVITIES

Writing Captions

Help your child collect any number of pictures from the paper and create original, funny, or exciting captions to go with those pictures.

Mystery Story

Invite your son or daughter to write a mystery story by cutting words and phrases from the paper and using those words to create the plot.

Rhyme Time

Encourage your child to write a rhyming poem using words found in the newspaper. Have him or her cut out the rhymed words and paste them in the appropriate spots on the poem.

Facts and Opinions

Locate an editorial in the newspaper. Have your child read the editorial carefully and highlight in yellow all of the facts used in the piece. Next, using a different colored marker, all of the opinions in the article are circled. Discuss together why the article is effective and how the argument is constructed.

Emotional Mobile

Your child picks an emotion such as happiness, sadness, fear, anxiety, or anticipation. Then have him or her search through the newspaper and find as many words as possible that relate to that emotion. A mobile that features all of these words can then be created for display.

Letter Writing Practice

Have your child look through the classified ads and find a job that is appealing. Then have him or her write a letter of application, showing why he or she is the best person for that job. A fictitious résumé that highlights one's qualifications for the chosen "dream job" also makes an excellent writing activity.

Comic Search

Scan the comic strips and suggest things for your child to find when reading them. For example, your instructions might look something like this:

1. Locate a comic strip that shows something you like to do.
2. Find a comic strip that has a character who is like you in some way.

3. Which comic strip shows something you would like to do when you get older?

Weather Language

Weather terminology makes for wonderful vocabulary lessons! Writers generally use extensive vocabulary to describe weather conditions—"the wind howled" or "the sky erupted" or "the snow blanketed." Your child can cut out these descriptive phrases and paste them on a poster or in a small journal. The child can draw illustrations to match these phrases. An older child can make a list of weather vocabulary and then use these words to describe other things unrelated to the weather, such as an "ice-cold" temperament, a "stormy" marriage, or a "sunny" smile.

SOCIAL STUDIES ACTIVITIES

State Search

With your child, look over the newspaper for a full week and see how many different states you can find mentioned. Your child then cuts out these references and colors in each of the corresponding states on an outline map of the country.

Political Leaders

Have your son or daughter find three political leaders mentioned in news stories, and note their names, titles, and country or state they represent. Encourage your child to do research on the Internet to find out more about each of these leaders.

Virtual Travel

Your child finds a news article about a foreign country. He or she then follows the news about that country for two weeks and sees how many facts can be gathered about the country from the articles. Invite your child to write a story about imaginary travels to this country or to create a travel brochure for someone wanting to visit this place. (Note: Students can also find more about their specific location by consulting additional resources such as the Internet. Students might find out the latitude and longitude, the location relative to other places, the economy or type of government of the country, or something about the language, customs, or beliefs of the country.)

Map Work

There are numerous maps in every issue of a newspaper. Your child should practice using maps while reading the accompanying articles. Students should be aware of the map title, the cardinal directions (north, south, east, west), the map scale, and any relevant map legends. In one fun mapping activity, students choose any two cities mentioned in the newspaper and, using a map, figure out how to drive from one to the other in the shortest possible time.

Charting the Weather

Your child can chart the day-to-day weather for a period of two weeks. At the same time, he or she can follow the five- or ten-day forecasts as reported in the newspaper. Have your child do this activity and then compare the actual weather to the forecasts and draw some conclusions.

Natural Resources

Your son or daughter should be aware of the issues about renewable and nonrenewable resources in today's world. Work with your child to accumulate articles that relate to each type of resource. Have him or her research issues about the environment and/or follow discussions about the environment in the weekly paper.

SCIENCE ACTIVITIES

Mr. Gadget

Have your child scan the newspaper to find pictures of products that did not exist twenty years ago. Encourage him or her to learn how they were invented and who invented them. Next, challenge your child to try to create a new invention—a machine, a robot, or anything! The invention can be created using pictures and by putting together two things in a new way.

Picture Perfect

Ask your child to look through the newspaper and find a picture of a pet that he or she would like to own. The student then writes an imaginary story about the new pet.

Weather Wonder

Using the weather maps and weather forecasts, the student plans a two-week trip to a new location. The plan should include details on exactly what to pack so that the traveler is well prepared for the weather!

Pollution Solution

Have your son or daughter follow and collect articles that relate to some sort of pollution. After a few weeks of research, a letter is written to the editor outlining his or her ideas for some solutions to the given pollution problem.

MULTIPLE SUBJECT ACTIVITIES

Propaganda Alert

Have your child keep track of the ads in the newspaper over a period of two weeks—and analyze the ads: To whom do they appeal? What are they selling? How effective are they? What words or messages make people want to buy the product? Students then pick a product and design an imaginary ad campaign for it, keeping in mind what makes an ad powerful.

Profit and Loss

Show your child how to read the stock market reports in the newspaper. Older students can compute the percentage of profit and/or loss for a specific stock or even play the "stock market game." Students are "given" $1,000 to "invest" in any stock they choose; at the end of a period of time, students see if they have made a profit on their chosen stocks.

Furnish a Room

Using newspaper pictures and ads, your son or daughter can design and furnish any room in the house. He or she can also determine the cost of the room renovation by using article information and ads to keep track of expenses.

Commercial Message

Have your child find an article in the paper about a new product for home, school, or office, and then write a commercial advertising this product. He or she can even tape the commercial and share it with the entire family.

Sports Reporting

Invite your child to choose any sports article and rewrite it as if he or she were at the event. Encourage the use of exciting words and descriptors that make the reader "see" the sporting event.

Food Feast

Your child can use articles and ads from the grocery section of the newspaper to design a special feast for an upcoming holiday, be it Thanksgiving, Christmas, or the Fourth of July. The approximate cost of the food for this meal is then calculated.

Newspaper Scavenger Hunt

Have your son or daughter create a newspaper scavenger hunt for a number of related items. These items can be related to an upcoming holiday, a season, or to a child's special area of interest. For example, in a summertime scavenger hunt, the student might be asked to find:

1. A food that people eat in the summer.
2. Something children like to play with in the summer.
3. A word that describes summer.
4. A picture of children doing something special on their summer vacation.

CHAPTER

7

RESEARCHING FOR ANSWERS

Research is the process of going up alleys to see if they are blind.
—Marston Bates

In this century, the ability to locate and utilize information is a necessary skill. In both our personal lives and our business endeavors, we are bombarded daily by knowledge and information that we must process in order to function. Information literacy is no longer a luxury but rather a survival skill. Students need to learn how to access information, how to process and evaluate that information, and how to engage in both problem-finding and problem-solving activities that will sustain them as lifelong learners. Research fosters independent learning, higher-order critical-thinking skills, and academic curiosity.

The teaching of research skills cannot begin too early. It is a process that students must learn, practice, and then reinforce at more and more complex levels of achievement. Parents can serve students of every age as resource partners; you can work with your child to help interpret the world and to discriminate among the mass of information sources that assail them on a daily basis. Using this chapter in conjunction with Chapter 8, "Using the Computer," will help you to prepare your child for the world of academia as well as for the business world.

Research begins with inquiry. It is important to train students not only to ask questions, but to be able to pose the right types of questions to lead them to the information they seek. After posing questions, students must learn how to do the actual research; they must learn how to read discriminately and how to document and record their discoveries. Finally, the end product of research is sharing one's findings and reflecting on the research process. This can be done in any number of ways as you will see in the pages that follow. Research is not a daunting task accomplished only by post-doctoral candidates in remote laboratories. What this chapter will demonstrate is that research can happen anywhere, at any time, and can be done by anyone needing answers to questions.

 ## *Preschool and Elementary Students*

As the parent of every young child knows, a young child's questions can be unending. Sometimes, parents wonder if asking "Why?" is the sole preoccupation of the preschooler. But do not despair. This is the first step in stimulating active learning and critical thinking. Every time your young child asks a "why" question, that child is engaged in the learning process. Active learning involves children in thinking and promotes discovery about the world. Parents can help these youngsters be self-directed and interactive by serving as a coach, mentor, and guide in this learning process. Many times, the answer to the "why" question is a collaborative experience that makes parents learners with their children.

When a preschooler asks a "why" question, that child is initiating a very basic step in the research process: the inquiry. The child has discovered a problem or has made an observation about the world, and wants to better understand that observation. The child wants to construct his or her own understanding of a problem in the youngster's own domain. A question about the atmosphere ("Why does it rain?"), or about one's environment ("Why did that bee sting me?"), or about a child's immediate world ("How does a letter get to Grandma's house?") creates a teachable moment in which to do authentic research.

For a child who is not yet reading, it is important for parents to model the research process and work with the youngster to acquire answers. Answering "I don't know but let's find out!" to a child's questions, makes parents and children collaborative researchers. Younger children are fascinated by the world that surrounds them, and it is very easy to encourage them to find out more.

Although young children love fiction stories, it is also important to expose them to nonfiction reading materials. (See Chapter 6, "Reading the Newspaper.") Reading informational texts (or having them read aloud) helps students' reading comprehension and helps them build an informational knowledge base that will serve for all future learning. For example, many young children seem to be fascinated by the animal world—from dogs to dinosaurs. When parents and children read together, particularly nonfiction, informational texts, there are a myriad of opportunities that arise for questions that can lead to research.

Witness the fascination younger children have with the dinosaur world and with stories about their favorite types of pets. Books or magazines about domesticated pets or wildlife can start students on a lifelong passion for reading. (There is a series of magazines called "Zoo Books" available, complete with illustrations and explanations that will appeal to children of all ages.) Parents can turn a young child's love of animals into a love of reading. Furthermore, these types of nonfiction accounts will challenge young children to learn more by doing further reading and research.

Any question can be the impetus for conducting research. Sometimes, if a child doesn't ask a specific question, a parent can provide a research experience by following up on an idea that was seen on television or in a movie. For instance, you might encourage young children to pick out an animal or something else that was authentic in a show or movie you viewed together. Next, you can help the child look up this thing on the Internet, in a magazine, or in an encyclopedia. Help children to read about how the real animal functions: what it eats, where it lives, and what its young are called, for example.

Observation is an important skill in research. Children can be shown how to use their senses and other tools to collect (and later, to record) information. Take, for example, the child who asks, "What do birds eat?" You can help that child come up with answers in several ways. Certainly, you can show the child where to go to look for the answers. However, there is another way to encourage the basic tools of scientific inquiry. Research should be structured for younger children into four major categories:

1. Asking the question/Observing phenomena
2. Gathering the information
3. Organizing the information
4. Sharing the information

For the youngest children, take a piece of paper and divide it into four sections as shown below.

QUESTION: WHAT DO BIRDS EAT?	*I think birds eat berries.* *I think birds eat cereal.* *I think birds eat grass.* *I think birds eat worms.*
Observation:	*I saw a bird eat a worm.* *I saw a bird drinking water from a fountain.* *I watched birds eating bird seed.*

Information:	Hummingbirds sip nectar from flowers. Birds swallow worms whole. Birds eat more than their body weight each day.
Summary:	Birds are big eaters. They eat more than their body weight each day. Birds eat worms, berries, and bird seed. Birds also drink plenty of water.

Head the first section with the "Question." In this case, it might be, "What do birds eat?" Under that section, the child can list what she has observed ("I saw a bird eat a worm,") or what she thinks may be the answer ("I think birds eat berries"). This is an elementary hypothesis.

Next, the child can be helped to gather information. This information might take the form of further observation (studying birds at a given time and place, or by building or watching a bird feeder) or it might be obtained online or in a book. The important thing here is that your child begins to observe and think critically about a given subject. As a parent, you can help your young child by writing down the observations and information obtained in answer to the question. These can be recorded in the second section of the paper, labeled "Information." For the older elementary student, the information/observations should be written on index cards so that they can be reshuffled into an organizational structure later on in the process.

The third step in the process is to organize this information. You can help youngsters by numbering the observations. For example:

1. The bird flew around the bird feeder.

2. The bird pecked at the bird seed.
3. The bird landed on a bush.
4. The bird ate a berry off the bush.

Finally, children should be encouraged to "publish" their findings; they can illustrate their reports by drawing or downloading pictures or by finding pictures in magazines. These pages should be put together into a booklike format and shared with other members of the family or with friends. The youngest of students can simply illustrate a single fact that they have learned. They (or you) can write the fact on a piece of paper and then draw a picture to match what they discovered.

Speaking of bird feeders, they make for wonderful initial forays into scientific research. Young children truly love to observe animals over a period of time. If you do not choose to have a bird feeder, consider getting a goldfish or other small animal. Even the family pet can be observed over a period of days or weeks. Choose a specific time of day to have your youngster do the observation. For younger children, it should be a time when you can help him or her note down the information. Remember, your job is to model the process for your child.

Another wonderful project for younger children is to help them create their own "zoo." You can begin by reading the Dr. Seuss book *If I Ran the Zoo.* If possible, a trip to a local zoo or wildlife park will help spur excitement for this project. Next, talk with your child about what type of zoo he or she might create if given the opportunity. You can then help your youngster find out about the different animals that might reside in this special zoo. For each animal, have the child find out what it looks like, what its young are called, where it lives, and what it eats. Also have your researcher find or draw a picture of each animal in the zoo. Children should organize the information so that each animal has its own page in the final "book" version of this report. With this activity, youngsters have not only asked and answered questions but also documented their findings and shared them with an audience. (Remember that even mom, dad, siblings or friends qualify as an authentic audience.)

Perhaps there is a particularly meaningful personal artifact in your home—one with which your child has expressed interest. It might be a photograph, a piece of artwork, a piece of jewelry, an urn, a medal or award given to a family member—almost anything at all that has a personal familial history. You can guide your child to do research about this item by helping him or her pose questions about the item and then seek answers to those questions. Some sample questions might be:

- Where did this item come from?
- How old is this item?
- Is there a story that goes with this item?
- Can we find another item like it if we search on the Internet?
- What can someone learn from this item?

Children find it fascinating to begin research from a "personal" perspective. They love to learn about things that make them unique and then to connect those personal artifacts with similar items in the outside world.

Once in elementary school, students start research as early as kindergarten. These youngsters learn to see themselves as researchers and writers having something worthwhile to articulate and then share with others. Kindergarteners study the same array of topics as do older students (science, history, social studies, language arts) and are exposed to primary sources via hands-on experiences. For example, kindergarten students might learn how early settlers made bread. They would hear about the history, and then set about making bread for themselves. Students might make and bake bread, eat different types of bread, and even visit a modern bakery to see how bread is mass produced. These are all forms of research; students learn to combine information with firsthand observation and then to think critically about that information.

Often the teacher directs the class in this research process, modeling the steps based on the readiness level of the children in the class.

However, in the older elementary grades, students will be expected to engage in independent research activities that will help them to construct their own understandings of different materials. Older children follow essentially the same steps as younger ones in initiating the research process; however, the steps will have greater details and the process itself may take a longer time. The expanded research steps for the older elementary (and middle school) student are as follows:

1. Choosing the topic.
2. Narrowing the topic. / Creating a KWL chart./ Asking the right questions.
3. Gathering information./Finding resources.
4. Taking notes and organizing the information.
5. Writing, revising, and editing the report.
6. Creating a bibliography or works cited list.
7. Sharing the final product.

Many of the above steps have been discussed in Chapter Two, "Writing to Learn." Students need to choose a topic that addresses the subject but is neither too broad nor too narrow to be used for the report. Students might want to create a "KWL chart" in order to help them narrow down the points to be researched. A KWL chart contains three columns:

1. What I know (about a topic)
2. What I want to know (about the topic)
3. What I learned (about the topic after my research)

K	W	L
What I know...	*What I want to know...*	*What I learned...*
Certain birds live at the North Pole.	Which birds live there? How do they survive? What do they eat? How do they raise their young?	Several species of birds live and breed far to the north. They have been spotted migrating toward the North Pole. Because they cannot lay their eggs or rear their young on ice floes or bergs, scientists think that these birds find land where they can raise their young. The Arctic tern is a small bird that makes the longest migration of any bird and breeds in the Arctic. These social birds live in large groups, called colonies. This bird flies over 21,750 miles each year. Arctic terns have a life span of about 20 years.

In the important second column, students can generate questions about the given topic in order to narrow the topic and focus the research.

A circle map is another way to narrow a topic and generate researchable questions. The student draws a circle and puts the research topic in the center of the circle. The student then writes as many questions as possible in the area surrounding the inner circle. Finally, the student chooses one or two of the most important or interesting questions and attempts to find answers through research.

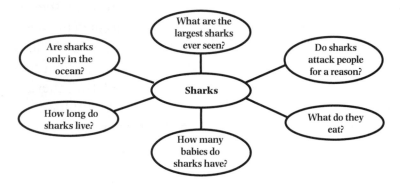

Students must learn how to find and use resources to locate information. When doing research, it is important for students to be aware that they should use multiple sources to find information. Given the availability and speed of today's computers, students naturally gravitate toward the Internet as their initial resource. There are many search engines appropriate and available for use by preschool and elementary school students. A list of many of these can be seen in the next chapter on using the computer. Students should also be encouraged to visit their school or local library or media center to avail themselves of other possible resources. Students who learn early on to use the reference section of a library or media center will find more sophisticated research far easier as they advance in their academic years. There is so much information available on any given topic that students may feel overwhelmed and not know how to extrapolate only the information that is needed. Students must be reminded that they should focus their information gathering on the initial research questions that they generated. Certainly, however, if they discover interesting points that they did not know before, they may choose to add additional questions or even change the focus of their research entirely.

As students read the information, they need to be critical and active readers. That means that they must consider what they are reading and discern the most important or main idea of the text. They must be reminded not to write down every bit of information and to try to record the information in their own words. If they do write something exactly as it is in a book, they should make certain to use quotation marks and to write down in parentheses where they got the information.

Middle School Students

Remember that research skills are cumulative. Middle school students will use the same skills as elementary students; they will ask questions, gather information, organize the information, and present that information. Naturally, this will be done at a more sophisticated level than in previous years. When a student enters middle school, he or she should be relatively comfortable with the basic research process. Students of this age group should have been exposed to online research as well as to the reference section of the school or local library. Students should be able to determine what sources in a library would most likely provide them with the best information for the topic they are researching. They should be familiar with the use of a basic Internet search engine, and know how to do a search using basic keywords. Students should also be comfortable using newspapers, periodicals, and magazines to access needed information. Middle school students will practice refining the research process; students need to learn how to sort and assess all of the information available and how to garner only the information that relates to their specific topic. Additionally, middle school students will practice outlining or other ways of organizing their information, and draft, edit, and revise a completed project. In the middle years, students are often asked to present an oral report on their findings; this is yet another aspect of the final research presentation. Learning to share research information effectively prepares students for the skills needed in any eventual workplace situation. Essentially, middle school students practice becoming increasingly effective at critical thinking and processing information.

Research at the middle school level teaches students to be self-directed learners. Students who are successful with the research process will become confident in their own ability to acquire knowledge; these same students will be enthusiastic about their learning and will be able to make connections between learning and the real world.

CHOOSING A TOPIC

Sometimes, teachers will give students specific areas in which to research, for example, The Pyramids, The Civil War, The Life of George Washington, or The Invention of the Rocket. The topics may even be narrowed to specifics: How Seat Belts Save Lives, The Cycle of a Hurricane, or "How to Grow a Tomato Plant." At times, however, students will be given free rein to create (and narrow) their own topics for research. In any of these cases, the process is pretty much identical. Students must take a subject and figure out how to develop it.

If the topic is not given by the teacher, there are a number of ways that students can go about generating ideas for subjects. First, of course, is to write about something that is interesting. If your child has a special interest or hobby, he will naturally find writing about that topic most exciting. However, let's suppose that your student is starting with a clean slate—no topic in mind. One way to proceed is to start with an encyclopedia or dictionary and make a list of topics that seem interesting. Here are a few general topics pulled from the dictionary:

- Art
- Baseball
- China
- Melt-down
- Sapphire
- Video

LIMITING THE TOPIC

Obviously, any of the above topics are far too general to manage for a research topic. The topics must be significantly reduced if students are to try to tackle research about the subject. Students need to learn how to limit a topic by considering one aspect of that topic. For example, for the first topic, "Art," students need to think about a specific kind of art (Modern Art), a specific time or place (Modern Art in Twentieth Century America), and a specific aspect of the topic ("How Modern Art in Twentieth Century America Changed American Values"). This process is a reduction game, and students should try to reduce the topic until it is of a sizeable proportion on which they can write.

The second topic, "Baseball," is far too extensive for a middle school research paper. Therefore, students must again reduce the topic to a workable size.

TOPIC: BASEBALL
LIMIT TO ONE LEAGUE: THE AMERICAN LEAGUE

(CAN'T WRITE ABOUT THE ENTIRE LEAGUE, SO....)

LIMIT TO ONE TEAM: THE NEW YORK YANKEES

(CAN'T WRITE ABOUT THE ENTIRE TEAM HISTORY, SO...)

LIMIT TO ONE YEAR: THE NEW YORK YANKEES
TEAM OF 1962

(CAN'T WRITE ABOUT THE ENTIRE YEAR, SO...)

LIMIT TO ONE EVENT: THE NEW YORK
YANKEES 1962 GAME AGAINST THE CHICAGO
WHITE SOX

(EVEN MORE SPECIFICALLY): LIMIT TO
ONE PLAYER: MICKEY MANTLE'S 1962
PERFORMANCE AGAINST THE CHICAGO
WHITE SOX

It is in this way—constant reduction—that one determines how to pose a topic for research. Once students locate and determine the subject for research, they must ask themselves a few more questions. The overall question should be, "What do I want to say about this topic?" As students answer this basic question, their initial hypothesis begins to form. For example, in the above example, a student might think, "I want to show that Mantle's performance in the 1962 game against the White Sox was the most important game of his career." This is an initial hypothesis that may change as the student begins the research. It is, however, most important to write down that initial thesis. Sometimes, students will need to do a bit of reading on the reduced topic in order to generate that initial hypothesis. Students are intrigued by "what-ifs," and these make for exciting and original thesis arguments. Students might pose questions such as "What if Mickey Mantle had not hit a home run in the World Series?" or historical what-ifs such as, "What if Columbus had never met Ferdinand and Isabella?" or "What if Martin Luther King had not marched in Birmingham?"

Next, students must ask themselves questions in order to organize a research plan. Students must decide:

1. What kind of research is needed?
2. What sources will provide me with the needed information?
3. Where should I go to gather the needed resources?

Remind students that sources might include the Internet, the library, biographical information, speaking with other people (interviews), magazines, newspapers, catalogs, or specialized journals. Finding information on Florence Nightingale will certainly lead down a different research path than researching Derek Jeter's family life or the latest findings of the Hubble telescope. Students also need to evaluate their information sources in order to assess the reliability of the information.

RESEARCH AT HOME

At home, parents can challenge students to find answers and do research by incorporating this activity into their immediate surroundings. For example, you might say to your youngster, "I wonder who invented the can opener. Do you think you can find out?" There are millions of household inventions that would serve as wonderful practice research pieces for middle school children. They might delight in discovering more about your telephone, air conditioner, frozen vegetables, sewing machine, zippers, safety razor, lightbulb, electric stove, DVD player, microwave—the list can go on and on.

Another at-home research project is to engage your child in helping plan the family vacation. Students are fascinated by travel to places near or far. Your child can become your "travel agent" and search for fun places to go and for amazing things to do once you are there. They can find information relating to places of interest, modes of transportation to get there, special events, places to stay, places to eat, and nearby sites to visit. Students can use the Internet, encyclopedias, magazines, travel books, maps, and an array of brochures to investigate these things.

Students are also fascinated by artifacts, particularly if they are personal ones from their own environment. Students can become detectives or scientists and learn about things from the past that have "traveled" into their own time and space. For example, a vase brought over by a great-grandparent from Europe could lead to all sorts of primary and secondary research experiences. An old photo can send students to historical sources to learn the how, when, and why of the photographed event.

Building an addition, installing a new window, or redoing the kitchen can all be occasions for research. Students can learn how an electrician wires a circuit, how a builder might use math to plan construction (or to determine construction costs), and how a decorator does an initial layout to plan where things will be placed. Inspiration for at-home research can be found wherever you look, and students can be encouraged to partner with you to learn these different things.

GATHERING INFORMATION: TAKING NOTES

Obviously, it is important to learn how to take good notes once information has been located. The Internet makes "cutting and pasting" an easy task, but, unfortunately, this technique often leads to a research paper that is partially or wholly plagiarized. Instead, students should learn to read the information and then *paraphrase* what they have read. Paraphrasing is restating the information in one's own words. It is different from *summarizing,* a skill that calls for reducing the information into its most basic or important context. Summarizing is a compression of ideas, while paraphrasing consists of putting all of the information into one's own words. Usually, students will use a combination of summarizing, paraphrasing, and even directly quoting information as they gather information. Students might want to consider using the Cornell Note-Taking Method explained earlier. Notes are taken in the right-hand column, main ideas are placed in the left-hand column, and on the horizontal area at the bottom of the page students may summarize the information. Each individual article or information source should have its own page if this method is used for research note-taking.

Notes can be taken in a variety of ways. Some students prefer to use an outline style of note-taking, while others simply write phrases about the information. Some students like to use a binder, some use a legal-pad, others use word-processing programs such as Microsoft Word and type notes directly onto the computer, while still others use index cards to jot down notes. The advantage to the index card system is that students can carry the cards to the library, whereas, unless they have a laptop computer, it is impossible to always use a computer in a public place. Furthermore, organizing the information is easily managed by manipulating and reorganizing the actual cards into a sequence that can be translated into a coherent, flowing paper. Whichever method is used, it is always imperative to separate the bits of information: one fact per sheet of paper or per index card—so that the organizational step can be managed with ease. Only by practice will students come up with the note-taking system that works for them.

PLAGIARISM

Middle school students are old enough to begin to understand the serious nature of plagiarizing. Plagiarizing is a crime and should not be done in any case whatsoever. Plagiarizing not only refers to stealing the exact words of another person without giving him or her credit for those words, but also involves the use of someone else's ideas without giving due acknowledgement. The latter point is a harder concept for students to understand. Sometimes, when students take someone's ideas and put them into their own words, they forget to credit the source of those ideas. Most students realize that if they use a direct quotation they need to use quotation marks and credit the originator of those words. However, students must also learn that when they use someone else's ideas or opinions (unless those ideas or opinions are common knowledge) they must give credit to that individual or source. Use the "wake-up test" to guide students in proper citation. Ask, "Did you wake up this morning knowing this fact?" If the answer is "no," the student may want to consider giving credit to the source of the information. Usually, students can use the following guidelines for crediting information. Give credit when using:

- someone's direct words or phrases.

- someone's ideas or opinions.

- facts, examples, or statistics that others have compiled.

WRITING THE PAPER

Having decided upon a topic, suitably narrowed it down, and then taken appropriate notes, the student must now decide how to best organize the information for writing and presentation. In other words, the smaller pieces of information must now be organized into a whole: the written paper. It is most helpful to begin the paper with an outline so that the details of the paper flow smoothly and logically from one idea to the next. The outline can be as detailed or basic as necessary; the essential component is the orderly flow of information.

Here is an example of a basic outline:

Topic: The Importance of Annie Sullivan in the Life of Helen Keller

Introduction: (This is the **thesis** or main hypothesis of the paper.)

If it were not for Annie Sullivan, Helen Keller would have led a far different life.

Body Paragraphs:

I. Background information on Helen Keller
  A. Childhood
  B. Cause of blindness
  C. Description of how she acted before meeting Annie Sullivan

II. Background information on Annie Sullivan
  A. Childhood
  B. Education
  C. Reason for working with Helen Keller

III. Day of first meeting—March 3, 1887
  A. How Helen reacted
  B. How Helen's family reacted
  C. First steps to teaching Helen

IV. Major Breakthrough
  A. Describe water incident
  B. Use information from Annie Sullivan and Helen Keller's writings
  C. Rapid education for Helen Keller after this incident

V. *Conclusion*: Explain how meeting Annie Sullivan totally changed the direction of Helen Keller's life.

Having written the outline, the student now sorts through the gathered information to match the order of the outline. This is why it is so important to put information on single sheets of paper or on index cards—at this point the information can be shuffled and reshuffled to make sense of the order.

Decisions have to be made about the order of the information presented. Sometimes, the logical sequence is rather obvious and the information almost puts itself in order. In the example outline, chronological order seemed best for proving the thesis. Other times, especially when one is comparing two or more things, the best order is not all that apparent. The student writer will have to determine if the report should be a paragraph-by-paragraph comparison or if the paper should first present one full component and then the next. Sometimes it is a matter of comparing likenesses first and then moving on to the differences. There is no single best way to compare two things; students will decide based on what makes the most sense to them. Every paper should have, however, an introduction to the subject matter, a hypothesis or thesis about the topic, body paragraphs that support that thesis, and a conclusion that ties all of it together.

Depending on the teacher, students may be required to do parenthetical citation (also called in-text citation) and/or a "Works Consulted" or "Bibliography" page. All these will be further explained in the next section for high school students. Briefly, these are simply a list of the books, magazines, Internet sites, films, journals, and so on, that were consulted or quoted in order to write the paper.

Students should be reminded that the first time they write a paper it is only a draft. They now must look over their work and check for accuracy. They should feel free to revise the paper—add or subtract information, fix punctuation, spelling, and grammatical errors—and recheck the accuracy of their information. Remind students that an excellent way of editing and revising papers is to read the paper aloud, making obvious corrections. Next, have a friend, sibling, or parent read the paper and suggest possible changes or additions.

Finally, the paper is ready for completion. The student might want to reflect about the ways that he or she may present the paper if an oral presentation is also required. The student may want to consider creating supplemental graphs, charts, PowerPoint presentations, or other visual aids to help the audience understand the researched information.

 ## *High School Students*

High school students will engage in varying amounts of research throughout their four years in school. High school research is meant to prepare students for higher-level academic research in college, graduate school, and the eventual workplace. Students at this age should be cognizant of all of the research procedures listed above; specific techniques and more sophisticated and analytical research will be practiced at this level. Primarily, high school students will be asked to write research papers to inform, to persuade, or to interpret information.

THE RESEARCH PROCESS: GETTING STARTED

The exact same research steps (on a substantially more sophisticated level) are required of the high school student as were required of the younger academician. First, the student must determine the subject and purpose of the research. Often, that will be determined by the instructor, although many do give students leeway to incorporate their own areas of interest. If at all possible, students should select a topic of interest, since they will most likely be working on the paper for a number of weeks, if not longer.

Older students should make it a point to avoid doing research solely on the Internet; more sophisticated papers require a wide variety of sources found in libraries and media centers. Students will use general reference books, biographical and autobiographical works, dictionaries, almanacs, subject-specific reference books, indexes, abstracts, government publications, and letters and journals, to name a few. High school students will be handling both *primary* and *secondary* source materials. Primary documents are "firsthand" sources: These are letters, diaries, firsthand accounts, original statistics, and books written on the topic by the author. Secondary sources are just that: commentaries, essays, and reports about a topic; analyses of a subject by an outside source; and interpretations of novels, plays, or even scientific information by analysts or critics. Students will have to learn the individual library's book catalog system; most of them are currently in an online format, although some libraries still have extensive card catalogs. Whether students access books, magazines, journals, or online sources, they will have to ask themselves to assess the information to see if it will be valuable to their specific paper. (Note: Chapter Eight explains how to evaluate an online Web site.) Students must consider whether the publication is current enough for their use and whether the author of the text is a reliable source for that topic.

A RESEARCH PLAN

Not unlike younger students, high school students need to take the time to think about and limit the topic of their research paper. Sometimes, the required length of the paper or the time allotted to complete the paper will help determine the scope of the topic. Too often, high school students procrastinate about starting research papers, leaving too few days to do what should have been accomplished over a period of weeks or more. Having your high school student write out a specific work schedule will help avoid the panic that usually ensues with night-before syndrome. Students cannot research and write an adequate paper in one night! Have the student plan specific dates and times for finding resources, for taking notes, for organizing and drafting the paper, and for writing the final version of the paper. In high school, teachers often set deadlines for students, giving dates to see their research, their notes, their first drafts, and their final copies. Remember, high school is simply a preparation for college work; professors only give students one "due date," leaving the time management issue to the student's own discretion. If students have learned how to manage their time for research in high school, the college research paper will flow far more easily.

TAKING GOOD NOTES

After finding and limiting a topic and finding appropriate resources, high school students must also take notes about their topic. The backbone of a good research paper is the accumulation of accurate, well-documented, and well-organized notes. Students need to think critically about a given text and consider how what they are reading will complement their given topic. Students should take adequate notes, without writing down each and every word of a text—unless they are quoting something specific. For every note taken, students should also record the author and source of the information; not only will this aid in citation work, but if one wants more information, the source can always be consulted again later in the process. Paraphrasing, summarizing, and direct quotations should all be noted carefully on the note cards. (A simple *P, S,* or *DQ* can be helpful distinguishing tools.) When students gather information, they should include as many varied sources as possible, including interviews or non-print media sources where relevant.

High school students will often research controversial issues. These issues might be anything from steroid use by high school athletes to handgun laws, free speech, student rights, or medical ethics. Students will have to understand why the particular topic is controversial and read varying opinions on each issue. Students doing this type of research will have to learn how to evaluate their sources for accuracy, reliability, currency, and applicability to their topic. When authors or other sources conflict with one another, students need to read critically and be able to understand the reason for the conflict. Students can learn to use conflicting sources without lessening the effect of the thesis of their own paper.

Sometimes high school students who are asked to do special interest papers (often called "I-search" papers) will be required to conduct a survey of sorts. Practice with surveys allows students to gain experience in authentic research and to mirror the process that "real" researchers often follow. Students will need to determine exactly what they want from the survey, decide how they want to design the survey, identify the population who will take the survey, and then collect and analyze the data from the survey. High school students will practice including both graphs and charts in their research papers; these can be from their own surveys or from a variety of published sources.

WRITING THE PAPER WITH PROPER CITATIONS

All of the information previously discussed in this book about the writing process comes into play with the writing of the research paper. Students use their information to write an outline, and then follow that outline and use the gathered information and notes to write the rough draft. The primary difference between writing a research paper and other types of writing is the use of citations— giving credit to the authors and sources of the information.

There are three main formats used for crediting sources of information: the *MLA (Modern Language Association)* style, the *APA (American Psychological Association)* style, and the *Chicago Manual of Style*. Students may be instructed by their teachers to follow a particular style. Many sources—books and Internet—delineate the exact specifications of each style. Whichever style a student selects, it is important that the paper be consistent. Both the MLA and the APA styles require students to use in-text citation rather than footnotes. These are also referred to as parenthetical documentation. Essentially, quoted or referenced sources are acknowledged within the paper—immediately following the quoted material—and keyed to an alphabetical "Works Cited" list at the end of the paper. For example, if someone were writing a research paper and quoting this book, the in-text citation would look like this in MLA style:

"The primary difference between writing a research paper and other types of writing is the use of citations—giving credit to the authors and sources of the information." (Weinthal 29). On the "Works Cited" page, "Weinthal" would be listed alphabetically with other information related to this particular book. The "29" in the citation explains that the information came from page 29 of the book written by Dr. Weinthal, listed on the "Works Cited" page.

Both the MLA and the APA styles require that the student compile a citation page. MLA calls it a "Works Cited" page, while APA refers to it as a "References" page. Both formats list all of the works used in the research paper alphabetically by authors' last names. Books, magazines, journals, and online sources listed in the works cited or references pages give information about the author, the full title of the text, the edition, the publisher, the date of publication, the number of pages, and other relevant information for the reader. High school students are fully aware of the ethics involved in lifting the ideas or resources of others without proper citation.

HOW YOU CAN HELP

After the paper is written, you can help your student by serving as another set of eyes to read through the paper. First and foremost, show interest in the topic chosen for research. Allow your son or daughter to become your "teacher," and get involved in the subject that he or she has selected. As you read the paper, keep in mind these guidelines for helping to edit the paper:

1. Identify the thesis of the paper, and make certain it makes sense. Has the student proved the main point?

2. Has the student fixed all of the mechanical errors of spelling and punctuation?

3. Have all of the sources been adequately cited?

4. Is the information presented in an organized fashion?

5. Does the paper need any additional information to make it clear?

6. Does the paper need to have any irrelevant information deleted?

7. Has the student met the requirements of the assignment?

The research process for most high school students can be reduced to ten steps. Naturally, as the student progresses in high school these steps become more and more sophisticated, and the skills are expected to become further refined.

TEN STEPS IN THE RESEARCH PROCESS

1. **Choose a broad topic:** Recognize and choose a researchable topic; (eventually choosing a topic that can lead to original concepts).

2. **Get an overview of the topic:** Read a variety of sources in order to get an overview of the topic; identify key issues.

3. **Narrow the topic:** Narrow the topics to a problem or question or focused point of view.

4. **Develop a thesis:** Construct a preliminary working thesis statement that can be supported by the research.

5. **Formulate questions to guide the research:** Formulate questions to probe and/or break down the topic (How? What? Where? Who? When? Why?).

6. **Plan for research:** Create a research and production plan including all deadlines.

7. **Find, analyze, and evaluate sources:** Locate essential information in a variety of resources (primary and secondary sources); analyze and evaluate those sources with regard to the working thesis.

8. **Evaluate evidence, take notes, compile a source file for citation:** Assess the accuracy of the information; take careful notes that answer the research questions; document direct quotations and record sources for summarized information; differentiate among facts, opinions, and values.

9. **Establish research conclusions and organize information into an outline:** Categorize information; develop an outline; determine how or why the evidence proves the thesis; develop an outline to guide the final product.

10. **Write the paper:** Draft, revise, edit the final product; use oral presentation skills to present the findings if necessary.

PRACTICING RESEARCH AT HOME

High school students are interested in topics that relate to their own lives as teenagers, as well as far-reaching problems that exist in the world. Parents can give teens research practice in a wide variety of at-home projects. Teens can help research and plan family vacations and outings, and they can help research major purchases for the home. Have your teen research the best brand of microwave or television, or have him or her help you investigate the computer that will best serve your family. In addition, high school students are particularly interested in career choices. The student may wish to investigate possibilities for a summer job, or possibilities for future employment. This inquiry can involve research, reading, interviewing, and other types of investigation. Career research will entail examining the skills necessary for a particular job, the type of education needed for the job, any certifications or state or national examinations necessary for the job, and the type of personality it might take to do well in a particular field. Students will also have to determine the demand for this career choice, and weigh the positive and negative aspects of the job.

Older students will also want to engage in research for their college choice. The same type of questions generated for a career investigation might be asked in a college search. Additionally, students will want to research the locale of the college, the types of students accepted, the notable specialties of the college, the requirements for admission, the cost, and the types of courses required of freshmen.

High school students often do mini-research projects without even realizing they are researching. Finding out the cheapest place to buy a particular DVD, the best place to go after the prom, and biographical information on their favorite celebrity are all forms of research. And when that all important moment arrives—getting one's driving license—you can be certain your teen will be happy to "research" the type of car he or she most desires.

When students become confident researchers, they feel capable and empowered to go through life learning about new things. They know that answers are out there if they can pose the correct questions, and they know that with the proper skills and much diligence, they can learn how to research the answers to those questions themselves. You can help your child learn analytical inquiry and build knowledge by serving as an at-home research collaborator and by making the world of research an exciting and stimulating family activity.

CHAPTER

8

USING THE COMPUTER

Technology does not drive change—it enables change.
—Anonymous

Computers, although not inexpensive, can be found in the majority of homes across America. In many cases, homes have multiple computers, more often than not hooked up to a wide variety of online Internet access programs. Parents have purchased computers, peripheral equipment, Internet services, and a multitude of computer accessories, with the expectation of having their children become active participants in the information age. At the same time, however, parents are also barraged by fears of unsafe or inappropriate Web sites for children, by certain educators who claim that the computer can stifle a child's creativity and innate curiosity to explore, and by the very real concern about Internet predators.

Parents want to help their children become technologically savvy and want them to learn to use the computer to genuinely further their intellectual growth—and with some parental guidance these goals can be achieved. If used correctly, the computer can be an exceptional tool to support a student's education, and it can be the element that provides the excitement to spark a child's desire to learn. Parents can make the best determinations of when a child has been at a computer long enough and when it is time to go out and play. Parents must also take responsibility for a child's safe engagement with Web surfing and work with their children to see that the computer is used appropriately to gain new information and insights. The U. S. Department of Education publishes a guide for parents for safe Internet use. This guide can be found at: *http://www.ed.gov/pubs/parents/internet/tips.html*

Preschool and Elementary School Students

In the February 2005 issue of *Parents* magazine, there was an article on "techno tots" (157–158). The article claimed that three out of four households with children under the age of six have computers, as do many preschool and day-care programs. The article shared a few caveats about tots and computers, however, and they are exactly what one might expect:

1. Software should be developmentally appropriate for the child's age. (Software for young children should be marked with an *EC,* for "early childhood," as designated by the Entertainment Software Rating board.)

2. Adults should be available to supervise the use of the computer.

3. There should be a balance between computer and non-computer activities in the life of a young child.

Unquestionably, used as a learning tool for reading, writing, and numbers, the computer can help increase readiness for school and can engage youngsters in activities that will assist them with critical thinking and learning skills.

For elementary students, the computer is a way of expanding their world; they can take virtual field trips to a myriad of places, they can become "time travelers" and learn about places and times in the past, they can "chat" with favorite authors or e-mail students in other countries, and they can speed up or slow down learning experiences to their individual pace.

For preschoolers, the computer is much like a toy; it has color and noise, and all the bells and whistles of a fancy game. As children move into elementary school, they need to learn how to use computers as tools of learning and they need to recognize that a computer can aid them in their day-to-day schoolwork. In many ways, computers can level the playing field for students of varying ability levels; computers aid students with organizational problems by providing graphic organizers and other ways to envision certain concepts. Furthermore, many computer programs have an oral component so that students with reading difficulties can hear as well as see text or program instructions. Parents can enhance in-school computer use by working at home with their children to use the computer for a multitude of instructional purposes.

Many encyclopedias are now available online and are a wonderful first stop for finding out specific information. Many times, these online encyclopedias also contain hyperlinked text that explains the words or phrases used in the articles and even provides links to further study about particular subject areas. You should put some or all of the following sites on your computer's "favorites" list and work with your child to access them frequently.

1. ***www.bartleby.com***   Comprehensive **online encyclopedia** and database of more than 51,000 entries; Columbia Encyclopedia Online

2. ***www.britannica.com*** (subscription)   another fine online encyclopedia

3. ***www.encarta.msn.com*** (Not free)   Microsoft Encarta is a comprehensive resource for accurate, up-to-date information. Encarta makes it easy to find information on nearly any subject.

4. ***www.encyclopedia.com*** This free resource offers more than 50,000 concise articles on a wide variety of subjects.

5. ***www.worldbookonline.com/***(subscription) Another online encyclopedia for access to articles for research.

6. ***http://www.wordcentral.com/*** (Merriam-Webster Online Student Dictionary) Look up word meanings, create a personal dictionary, and learn the "buzz word" of the day at this dictionary Web site.

7. ***http://grammar.ccc.commnet.edu/grammar/*** (Guide to Grammar and Writing) For help with any grammar questions or style/writing questions, check this site first!

8. ***http://www.smartkidssoftware.com/jnpdi1g.htm*** (Plumb's Visual Thesaurus) A fun way for students to look up synonyms, antonyms, and word meanings. (Not free)

9. ***http://www.factmonster.com/*** (Fact Monster) Fact Monster is the largest free reference site just for kids! Get homework help and find **facts** on thousands of subjects.

10. ***www.bv229.k12.ks.us/bvideas/resources/elemed.htm*** This is an incredibly large site for links to all types of elementary education topics and Web sites. A must-see for parents of elementary school children.

There are also a great number of "safe" search engines to help parents assist youngsters in finding correct information. These sites are excellent resources for teaching students how to find information and have the added advantage of limiting accessibility to Web addresses that are unsafe or may not be kid friendly. Some of these include:

1. Yahooligans:

http://yahooligans.yahoo.com/

An entire Web guide for youngsters with fun games, resources, movies, jokes, and anything else you can imagine.

2. Ask Jeeves for kids:

   http://www.ajkids.com/

   The fastest and easiest place for students to find answers online.

3. Kids Net

   http://www.kidsnet.org/

   KIDSNET helps children, families, and educators intelligently access the educational opportunities available from television, radio, and multimedia sources. If you need to investigate information related to children's programs, this is the place to start.

4. Kids Click

   http://kidsclick.org/

   This site is an annotated searchable directory of Web sites created for students by librarians. It is searchable by subject, reading level, and degree of picture content.

5. Awesome Library

   http://www.awesomelibrary.org/

   This site organizes K–12 education resources, including the top 5 percent for teachers, students, parents, and librarians.

6. Education World

   http://www.education-world.com/

   This is a multifaceted site that is a virtual doorway into educational resources. It is one of the most complete education sites on the net.

7. EduHound

   http://www.eduhound.com/

   Another fabulous site for educational resources, projects, and lessons—in every subject area!

8. Kid Safe Search at Google

   http://www.google.com/help/customize.html

   This site lets parents customize the search engine for safe surfing by students.

9. Gateway to Educational Materials

   http://www.thegateway.org/

   The Gateway to Educational Materials^{SM} is a Consortium effort to provide quick and easy access to thousands of educational resources found on various federal, state, university, nonprofit, and commercial Internet sites.

10. LookSmart's Kids Directory

    http://search.netnanny.com/?pi=nnh3&ch=kids

    The Net Nanny Kids Directory is a listing of over 20,000 kid-friendly Web sites that were vetted for quality.

    Looking for a "homework helper"? The amazing variety of educational Web sites can be invaluable tools for your youngster— and for you, if you are helping them! Some sites that might come in handy when helping with homework include:

1. WebMath (for help with math problems)

2. Exploratorium (great for all kinds of science information)

3. DiscoverySchool.com (an amazing and unending source of information for parents and students)

    How do you know if you have located a reliable, safe Web site? One learns very quickly that virtually anyone can publish anything on the Web. It is often very difficult to determine whether a Web source is credible or not. There are, however, a few guidelines that can help you and your child in this process.

Criteria for Evaluating Web Sites

There are a number of basic criteria used by academics to evaluate the reliability and usefulness of Web resources. Initially, parents will have to serve as the evaluators of these sites; however, children as early as kindergarten can begin to recognize some of the important tenets of Web site evaluation.

1. What is its purpose?

Web pages serve many purposes. When you use the Internet to execute a search for something, it is important to understand the purpose of the page that you discover. Naturally, some pages will have more than one purpose, but it is important to determine this so that the perspective of the information becomes clear. Some of these purposes will include:

- **Entertainment**: games, music, videos, films

- **Commercial Use**: a business trying to sell something on the Web, or a company trying to promote itself on the Web

- **Educational Purposes**: exists to teach something, to explain something, or to reference something

- **Persuasive Purposes**: exists to persuade the audience to its point of view

- **Personal Purposes**: a Web page constructed by an individual or group to record personal observations, comments, pictures, and so on

- **Institution**: an institution such as a school, a university, or a hospital may post a page that references its existence and its specializations and resources

- **Informational Purposes**: exists to provide information about a particular key word; many museums have these types of sites, as do towns and governmental offices

The URL (or the Web address) can often help you determine the purpose of the Web page. This is also known as the domain for the page. For example, a URL that ends in *.edu* will indicate that it is an educational institution's Web page. A URL that ends with *.com* is usually a commercial site, while a *.gov* is indicative of a government agency. When a page ends with *.org* it is usually an organization or professional group, while *.mil* is used only for the military.

2. Who are its authors?

You must always be observant and take note of the author or authors of a given Web page. Asking a few key questions can help determine author authenticity. You should be able to answer "yes" to most of the following:

- Does the author have respectable credentials or authentic corporate or organizational connections?
- Is the author clear about his or her purpose, and is borrowed information properly cited so that one can check the original information?
- Does the page describe a way to contact the author? Is there an e-mail, address, or phone number?
- Is the author someone who may have a bias or is the information presented in an equitable manner?
- Does this site provide other credible links?
- Did you link to this site from another known, reliable page?
- Does the author use factual information rather than emotion to display and disseminate the information?

3. Is the material current, relevant, and appropriate for your child's age group?

First, you must determine if the information on the Web site is up to date. Web sites that are reliable always state the date that the page was last updated. Since our world of information is changing so rapidly, it is imperative that students access the most current information available on any given topic. It may also be important to check on the date the information itself was gathered, as well as the date the page was updated. A student needs this knowledge for some types of information.

There is so much information on the Web that students doing research need to continually ask themselves if the content of the Web page is relevant to the subject they are researching. Irrelevant topics can simply interrupt the research process and throw students into a scavenger hunt that wastes valuable research time and energy.

Finally, you must decide if the Web page information is appropriate for your child's age and reading level. Not only must the content itself be appropriate, but your child should be able to understand the words and concepts on his or her own without much interpretation from you. The information should be clearly presented in a logical, well-organized, legible format without any obvious errors of spelling, punctuation, or word usage.

4. How are the technical and visual aspects of the Web site?

These aspects can also be analyzed by asking yourself a few important questions.

- Observe how the Web site loads to your computer. Does it take an inordinate amount of time to load, or is the process fairly simple?
- Are there clearly labeled pictures, charts, or other graphic elements that add clarity to the information on the page?
- Is the text on the page in a readable format with headings, subheadings, or other key points for readability?
- If there are pages or links to click on the page, do they all work?
- Do the links lead back to the home page?

■ Is there purposeful use of color and graphics, and do these graphics also download quickly?

■ Is the site interactive and do these activities engage the student?

Once a Web site is evaluated and deemed useful, it should be bookmarked so that the student can revisit it throughout the research process.

WORTHWHILE COMPUTER ACTIVITIES FOR YOUNGER CHILDREN

What kinds of activities can parents promote with the assistance of the computer? Below are some suggestions for Internet activities for the elementary school student.

Educational Games

Hundreds of sites on the Internet, dedicated to preschool and elementary school students, exist to enhance the young child's facility with basic reading, writing, and math skills. The activities on these sites are often formatted as games: story-boarding, filling in letters for accurate spelling, working out problems in addition, subtraction, division, and multiplication, to name a few. Games like Scrabble, various crossword puzzles, word searches, and word hunts can be found on multiple Web sites. Parents can download free reading games from numerous educational Web sites. Games that teach reading, spelling, and even literary analysis are available on Web sites for kids. These educational activities are cleverly disguised as games, and students will stay focused while learning through play.

Elementary Research

Parents can design a type of "Web quest" for their child to provide practice doing elementary research. This will require a topic and a few preselected Web sites that are given to the student. The student then visits those Web sites and locates the requested information. Students can then learn to open a document in a word processing program and type the acquired information into a document.

E-Pals

Your child can be encouraged (with your knowledge and input) to engage in an e-mail exchange with another youngster. This should, obviously, be someone with whom you are acquainted. There are some online sites that are specifically organized so that teachers can set up e-pals; these sites are very carefully monitored and secured so that students are not put in jeopardy. At home, e-mail should be confined to known acquaintances. E-mail can be a wonderful way to get students writing and communicating with an authentic audience. However, it is imperative to wait until children understand the danger inherent in e-mailing a relative stranger. Students need to be taught not to give anyone their address, phone number, or other personal information, and they must be trained to show you all correspondence of this nature. Students must understand that online relationships are not "real" the way person-to-person relationships are; they must be carefully taught Internet safety.

Author Correspondence

Students can also be encouraged, with your assistance, to write letters or notes to their favorite author. Most authors or publishers have Web sites where, most often, a link for students to correspond in some way with the author can be found.

Writing Reviews

Students can also be shown how to write film or book reviews and post them to the Web. Many kid sites have links so that students can "review this book" or "review this film." The authenticity of this project can make students enthusiastic readers and writers.

Weather Charting

Students can be encouraged to check the weather at one of the weather information sites. Older elementary students can check the weather in different locales—particularly if friends or family do not live nearby. Some students may want to keep weather charts and update them on a daily or weekly basis; this is another basic project that can set the tone for later scientific research techniques.

Creating Web Pages

There are many sites that are either "kid-authored" or contain links and instructions so that students may create their own Web page. There is one site, for example, called the "My Hero Project," which allows children to create their own Web page about someone who is a hero to them. Kid News is a site that has articles written by students for students. This allows students to hear the opinions of others their age and to read information in a language with which they identify.

Seeking Out News

Many of the news sites specifically for children also contain numerous online activities to go with their articles. Students can go online to find out about current issues in the news and then engage in activities to reinforce the concepts and information learned.

Reading Online

Students can even read poetry or fiction online. Some sites also have an oral component, so that pre-readers can hear the books read to them right from the computer. In fact, students can find the full text version of many books, from picture books to the works of Shakespeare, with a relatively easy search.

Trip Planning

Parents can work with students to find maps and directions on the Internet. Before you take a ride or a trip, investigate MapQuest or Maps On Us to locate and plot out the trip. County, country, and world maps are just a click away, and children can get a sense of their world by envisioning where they are in relation to places abroad.

Word Search

Students can be shown how to find the meanings or origins of words at Dictionary.com or at Merriam-Webster OnLine. They can be given a new word daily and keep a record of all the new words learned that week. Have your child create a mini-dictionary that he or she can illustrate with original drawings or with computer-generated graphic images.

Question Research

Challenge your child to find information by posing a "question of the week." Reward students when they find the answers; this mini-research can become a household game.

 # Middle School Students

Middle school students should be relatively proficient at computer use. Most have been using computers in the elementary schools and at home for quite a number of years. At this level, students should be comfortable with executing basic keyword searches, be familiar with some of the more common resources on the Web, understand the basics of Web page evaluations, and know how to use and retrieve information in coordination with a basic word processing program. The middle school student is also most likely familiar with PowerPoint and has probably already been asked to do a basic in-school presentation using this program. The task for middle schoolers is to refine all of these computer skills and to achieve a greater level of sophistication in the use of all of the above. As parents of middle school children, you will want to be aware of the places on the Net your child "surfs" and, in general, of the tasks he or she is completing while sitting at the computer. There are also a number of activities that you can initiate that will encourage thoughtful use of the computer by your middle school student.

LEARNING PROPER "NETIQUETTE"

Students are now old enough to understand that there are certain rules—unwritten as well as real legal issues—that come with Internet use. These should be reviewed with your child, and it should be made clear that along with independent Internet use comes the responsibility for using the Net wisely.

E-mail

Sending an electronic message, unlike a face-to-face encounter, does not allow for facial expressions or body language. Therefore, e-mail messages should avoid using all capital letters (which indicates shouting), saying something critical that would not be said to a person's face, and using sarcasm or humor that may be misinterpreted by the recipient.

Copyright Regulations

As discussed in the chapter on research, plagiarism (the use of someone else's ideas or exact words) is never allowable. Students should use their abilities to summarize and then give proper citation or credit to the source of the borrowed information.

Software Use

Copying or using "pirated" software is not acceptable. There are specific laws guarding against the use of software that has been obtained without proper payment.

Personal Information

Students should be wary of giving any personal information (name, address, phone number) to anyone via e-mail or in a chat room. Students should also understand the implications of using a credit card to buy something over the Internet; obviously, this should be done only with your express approval.

You should familiarize yourself with a wonderful site called *childrenspartnership.org*. Not only does this site offer significant information for parents beginning the journey through cyberspace, but it links to the *Parent's Guide to the Information Superhighway: Rules and Tools for Families Online* by Wendy Lazarus and Laurie Lipper (1998). The guide is downloadable, for free, and offers an incredible array of information for parents. It also includes a "contract" that students complete for safe Internet searching. This is an excellent way to have students consider the components of Web safety in a totally personal way.

As a parent, you need to set specific rules and regulations for computer use. Only you can decide what is and what is not acceptable use for your child. Be careful not to think of the computer as a babysitter; students do lose track of time and can sit at a computer for hours on end. Also, make certain that your son or daughter knows exactly what your rules are with regard to chat rooms, accessing pornographic sites, or even playing computer games.

SUGGESTED ACTIVITIES FOR THE MIDDLE SCHOOLER

Here are some ideas for some worthwhile family computer time projects.

Word-A-Day Challenge

Using the multitude of online dictionaries, your child searches (daily or weekly) for the meaning and possibly the derivation of a given word. This is a task that not only builds vocabuary skills but also encourages language research practice.

Meanings of Names

Students are fascinated by the meaning and etymology of their first and last names. There are many sites that they can visit to research this information. One particularly fun site is *www.behindthename.com*.

This site offers students information about the origin of their first and/or last names and provide other links to additional etymological information.

Word Games

Many students enjoy playing word games. At *www.wordfocus.com*, your child will find word definitions, vocabulary worksheets, lists of oxymora (contradictory or incongruous words) and pleonasms (redundancies), and Latin and Greek word derivations.

Internet Scavenger Hunt

Parents can devise an Internet scavenger hunt for middle school students. Give your child a list of people or things and see how much accurate information he or she can discover on the Web. Students should try to download pictures to accompany their discoveries and share their findings with family members.

Strange Phrases Make Great Internet Fun

Direct your child to *www.funbrain.com/funbrain/idioms/* or to *www.idiomsite.com* where he or she can play games while learning idiomatic expressions. Invite your child to copy down these expressions and then illustrate each with an original, comic drawing. For example, the phrase, "apple of my eye" has a specific derivation that students can discover. That particular phrase might be illustrated with apples where the eyes belong perhaps. This activity builds vocabulary and enhances reading comprehension while students are actually having fun!

Making Invitations and Greeting Cards

There are many sites available online for purchasing and sending e-cards. Several also offer a wide array of free cards and postcards. Instead of using these sites, however, have your child design his or her own greeting card, practicing downloading images from the Web and combining them with his or her own words. These cards can be printed on a word processing program and sent via snail mail or e-mail to recipients.

Movie Madness

Either before or after seeing a wonderful movie (either on television or in the movie theater) have your child visit the Internet Movie Data Base (*www.us.imdb.com*).

This site allows students to search by movie title, character, or even by a word or famous line from the film. Your child can find out all kinds of information about a given movie: title, genre, runtime, language, color, sound mix information, goofs, famous lines, and user comments. The site also offers unlimited links to all kinds of information related to film; for every person in the cast, there is a link to further biographical information about that actor.

Download and Use Graphic Organizers

Graphic organizers, as stated earlier in this book, are wonderful tools for helping all students get and stay organized. Parents can type in "graphic organizers" in a search engine like google.com and find an array of related sites. If you visit *http://www.eduplace.com/graphicorganizer/*, you will find an exceptionally large offering of graphic organizers that can be downloaded for student use. Remember that these tools can be used across the disciplines so that students can access information visually to supplement understanding.

Explore a Museum on the Web

Take your child on a museum exploration! Almost all of the major museums have Web sites where students may take a "virtual" trip through the museum. The same is true for art galleries and zoos. Students can sign on as a museum visitor and access pictures of major exhibits, artwork, displays, and other museum information. Many of these sites are also interactive, with games and activities that can help students hear and see as if they were actually there in person. Check out the National Smithsonian Museum for an unusual and worthwhile viewing experience. At *www.exploratorium.edu*, parents and students can access exhibits from the San Francisco interactive science museum, known on the Web as the "Museum of Science, Art, and Human Perception." All kinds of online experiments and challenges are available to students from this Web site.

Riddles and Other Games

At *www.eduplace.com* , students are given links to several types of games when they click the subtitle "edugames." Six amazing games that challenge students in spelling, geography, vocabulary, proofreading, and grammar practice can be found on this site. In addition, there is a section devoted to "brain teasers," giving students a weekly math word puzzle to solve. Parents can play these games with their children, and these can become a whole family activity.

There is no doubt that computers are here to stay. Remaining aware of your child's Internet activities can be a daunting task, but it is one that must be pursued with diligence. The best way that you can help is to model good computer habits for your children. Parents need to become learners *with* their children; spending time with your child while he or she is on the Internet fulfulls this goal and, at the same time, allows you to monitor his or her Internet activities. Remember, the computer is simply a tool and can't make your child a super-student alone. It also takes your time and effort to help students become critical thinkers and learners while they learn to master the skills needed for information literacy.

 ## *High School Students*

High school students should have all of the technological proficiencies of elementary and middle school students and will practice these skills at a more sophisticated level. For the high school student, computer use now prepares for the advanced technological skills that will be used in college and in the workforce. Students should be very familiar with Web searching and search engines, key word searches, bookmarking favorite pages, and virus protection tools. They should also be familiar with sending and receiving e-mail, and all of the associated e-mail etiquette. Students should understand the nature of passwords, and know how to protect their sensitive and personal information. Finally, students should be critical readers of Internet information, knowing how to best evaluate an informational Web page. In short, high school students are on their way to becoming official citizens of the World Wide Web.

Aside from personal use (e-mail, computer games, blogging) teens should be using the computer to help with their schoolwork. Students will find that the Internet is a rich resource for information for research papers and smaller reports, for job opportunities and internships, for inquiries about colleges and universities, and for help in just about any subject area they may be studying. Teens will naturally not want parental involvement in their Internet activities; parents need to find ways to still remain informed about their child's computer activities. Your son or daughter should still not be spending inordinate amounts of time solely on the computer; teens need a balance of diverse indoor and outdoor activities in order to be well rounded. The following are some ideas that can bring parents and teenagers together in the online world.

In-House Research

Ask your teens for help researching topics of familial interest; really listen to the information that they find so that they feel validated and empowered as "research assistants." They can help research information for your vacations or purchases, for example.

Online Writing Labs

Online writing help is available for short or long papers through one of the many "online writing labs" (OWL) that have recently been developed. Many of these writing labs have tutors who are willing and able to discuss varied aspects of writing with your student; most have tutorials that will answer all kinds of questions about composing and publishing. Two of these that are extremely well-known are sponsored by Purdue University and the University of Michigan. Students should learn to use these resources rather than panic when faced with an involved writing task.

Publishing on the Web

Whether students write and submit to an online magazine or journal, or simply post their writing on their own Web page, there is nothing more encouraging for a young writer than to see his or her work "out there." Encourage your son or daughter to submit finished writing, and you may see the beginnings of an enthusiastic writer and confident thinker.

Online Newspapers

Encourage your child to read a daily or weekly paper on the Internet. Teens need to be knowledgeable about events in the outside world; the Internet is the fastest and most convenient way for them to do this. As you may remember from the chapter on "Reading the Newspaper," becoming a critical reader, writer, and thinker requires current and knowledgeable information. Parents want to create positive, lifelong habits in teens, and one of these is becoming a perceptive citizen. Local and world-wide news is always available on numerous Web sites, and reading one or more of these on a routine basis is the best way for news reading to become a lifelong habit.

Listservs of Interest

Have students find a listserv about their hobby or about another topic of interest. With thousands of "discussions" on the Net daily, students can certainly find a list of interest to them. Have students subscribe to one of these lists and he or she will learn how to become part of a specialized Internet community.

Internet Scavenger Hunt

Students can be challenged (and even timed) to try to find answers to specific questions by using Internet search tools. Ask questions like, "What was the first Shakespearean play performed on American soil?" or "Which poem did Maya Angelou recite at Clinton's inauguration?" These queries can teach important research skills that will serve your child well in college.

Quotation of the Day

Use Internet quotation sites to find and post a "quotation of the day" on the refrigerator door. Or, perhaps you can suggest a specific topic and challenge your child to find an appropriate related quotation. Finally, if you come up with a quotation, invite your child to discover its source.

Resources for Online Research: A Beginning List

What follows is a list of some of the better-known Internet sites that will allow you and your high school student to begin to use some of the vast sources available in cyberspace. Remember, this is only a beginning. As you learn to surf the Web, you and your child will find many other sites that intrigue, challenge, and inform. Remember to surf wisely and safely and the whole world will be open to you.

SEARCH ENGINES:

AltaVista: *http://altavista.digital.com/*
Ask Jeeves: *http://www.askjeeves.com*
Excite: *http://www.excite.com*

Google: *http://www.google.com*
HotBot: *http://www.hotbot.com/*
Infoseek: *http://infoseek.com/*
Lycos: *http://www.lycos.com/*
Webcrawler: *http://www.webcrawler.com/*
Yahoo!   *http://www.yahoo.com/*

GENERAL DIRECTORIES:

Eric Clearinghouse: *http://ericir.syr.edu/*
Site for Educational Resources Clearinghouse.
Internet Public Library: *http://www.ipl.org*
A directory of Web information.
InfoSurf: E-Journals and E-Zines:
http://www.library.ucsb.edu/mags/mags.html
Lists of electronic magazines and electronic journals.
Listserv Lists Search: *http://tile.net/listserv/*
Lists of e-mail discussion groups.
Supreme Court Decisions: *http://www.law.cornell.edu/supct/*
Recent Supreme Court Decisions can be found on this site.
WWW Virtual Library:
http://www.w3.org/pub/DataSources/bySubject/Overview.html
A directory of Web sites.

DESKTOP REFERENCES AND SPECIALIZED WEB SITES:

Bartlett's Familiar Quotations:
http://www.cc.columbia.edu/acis/bartleby/bartlett/
CIA World Factbook: *http://odci.gov/cia/publications/factbook/*
Facts about countries of the world.
Merriam-Webster Dictionary: *http://www.m-w.com*
An online dictionary site.
Dictionary: *http://www.dictionary.com*
An online dictionary site.

Elements of Style:
http://www.cc.columbia.edu/acis/bartleby/strunk/
Resource for English grammar.
Grammar and Style Notes:
http://www.english.upenn.edu:80/jlynch/grammar.html
A grammar and writing style guide.
Quotations: *http://www.starlingtech.com/quotes*
Find quotations using a keyword search.
Roget's Thesaurus:
http://humanities.uchicago.edu/forms_unrest/ROGET.html
PEN: *http://www.pen.org/*
Home page for the professional association of writers and editors.
Perdue Online Writing Center: *http://www.perdue.edu*
Online help for writers; multiple writing tutorials available.
Research Papers: *http://www.researchpaper.com/*
Specific help with research papers.
Writing Centers Online:
http://departments.colgate.edu/diw/NWCAOWLS.html
A directory of online writing centers.
WWW Scribe: *http://www.wwwscribe.com/*
About writing for the Web and using the Internet as a research tool.

VARIOUS WEB SITES FOR THE HIGH SCHOOL STUDENT:

Authoring: *http://www.kidauthors.com/*
A site for students to submit or read all types of writings including poetry from fellow students; also contains advice for parents and links for stories, poems, puzzles, and games for students.
Bartleby – Columbia University: *http://www.bartleby.com/66/*
This "must-visit" site links to multiple text sites from quotations to *Gray's Anatomy* to the *Farmer's Almanac*.

Citation Help: *http://citationmachine.net/*
This incredible site makes creating proper citations fun. Just plug in the information and you are ready.

Consortium on Reading Excellence: *http://www.corelearn.com/*
Provides links to all kinds of information on reading and research on reading.

Current Events:
http://www.csun.edu/%7Ehcedu013/cevents.html
Wonderful starting site for teaching current events in newspapers, magazines, and TV; links to many other useful current event sources.

Discovery School: *http://school.discovery.com/info/aboutus.html*
Teaching materials, student resources, advice for parents on different aspects of learning and helping students enjoy the learning process.

Games, Games, and More Games:
http://trivia.games.myway.com/index.asp
Site with free games, including some on history, sports, music, and general knowledge trivia. Fun to play for kids or adults!

Government: *http://www.fedworld.gov/*
A searchable site of thousands of pages for information on the federal government and on government Internet sites.

Graphic Organizers: *http://www.eduplace.com/graphicorganizer/*,
http://www.enchantedlearning.com/graphicorganizers/vocab/
Sites for downloadable graphic organizers for every possible subject area.

Homework Help: *http://www.homeworkspot.com/*
Site for homework help in anything, including science, math, language arts, and history; has K–12 links for all students.

Internet Activities: *http://www.fno.org/feb97/teach.html*
Interesting articles for parents, with many suggested Internet activities to do with youngsters.

Learning Articles: *http://www.funderstanding.com/theories.cfm*
Site has many different articles about learning, critical thinking, assessment, and emotional intelligence.

Learning Styles:
http://www.engr.ncsu.edu/learningstyles/ilsweb.html
Take a learning style survey—find out your preferred learning style. Results are returned immediately.

Library of Congress: *http://lcweb.loc.gov/*
This site locates the Library of Congress' online resources.

Marco Polo: *http://www.marcopolo-education.org/about/about_index.aspx*
A consortium of national and international educational organizations providing K–12 educational information, including student resources, lesson plans for teachers, and numerous links to other educational Web sites.

Movie Information: *http://www.us.imdb.com/*
A huge database for searching anything and everything about the movies.

NASA: *http://www.nasa.gov/home/index.html*
A Web page gateway for NASA space exploration information; games and activities for younger kids, and information and resources for older students, educators, and researchers.

National Council of Teachers of Mathematics:
http://illuminations.nctm.org/index.asp
Comprehensive and interactive tools for learning and teaching math—a must-see for help with all pre-K–12 math questions; links to hundreds of interactive sites for practice with math problems.

National Organization for Women: *http://www.now.org/*
Starting point for research on issues for women.

National Council of Teachers of English:
http://www.ncte.org/
Tremendous array of information and archived articles about the teaching of English and literature.

News Sites: *http://www.cnn.com/, http://foxnews.com/, http://wwwnytimes.com/, http://wwwusatoday.com/, http://wwwwashingtonpost.com/*

Wonderful sites for reading the daily news. Some require subscriptions; others are available free online.

OWL from Perdue: *http://owl.english.purdue.edu/workshops/pp/*
Specific PowerPoint presentations related to writing instruction.

Poems Daily: *http://www.poems.com/*
Provides daily poems with links to a "featured poet" and to other poetry sites.

Poetry—American: *http://www.english.uiuc.edu/maps/poets.htm*
Features American poetry with poems and poets listed alphabetically; links to companion sites.

Quotations: *http://www.heartquotes.net/Becoming.html*
Wonderful site for retrieving quotations—and a great source for "quotation-of-the-day."

Read, Write, Think: *http://www.readwritethink.org/index.asp*
One of the most important English Language Arts sites for students, teachers, and parents; thousands of links to sites with student interactive materials and Web resources for almost anything of value for K–12 language arts materials. Endorsed by the National Council of Teachers of English.

Research: *http://www.sscnet.ucla.edu/library/*
Students can log in as a "guest" to this UCLA Web site and get valuable information and help on doing research.

San Diego County Office of Education:
http://www.sdcoe.k12.ca.us/score/cyk3.html
This site provides "cyber guides" K–12 for additional work with specified fictional readings; wonderful to use with any language arts curriculum.

Smithsonian Museum page: *http://www.si.edu/*
With so many links to a myriad of materials, it is like taking a trip to the real Smithsonian!

Study Skills: *http://www.bucks.edu/~specpop/Actfrm.html*
Links to a large array of sites specifically highlighting a variety of study skills; includes articles on all areas of study skills, including

reading, note-taking, listening, writing essays, memory aids, test taking, and many other specialized topics.

Teachers and Parents:
http://www.teachersandfamilies.com/open/parent/index.html
Site developed by teachers for students and parents with K–12 learning resources.

Teach-nology: *http://teachers.teach-nology.com/index.html*
Hundreds of downloadable practice sheets for all levels of students in many different subject areas.

United States Information: *http://www.census.gov/*
Information and a huge amount of statistics on all aspects of the U.S. population.

Web Quests: *http://webquest.org/*
Multiple samples of Web quests that students or parents can download and complete.

Words: *http://www.wordfocus.com/*
English vocabulary words derived from Greek and Latin sources.

SUGGESTED READING

PRESCHOOL–KINDERGARTEN

"Let's Get a Pup!" Said Kate by Bob Graham

1 2 3 by Tom Slaughter

100 Days of Cool by Stuart J. Murphy

A Chick Called Saturday by Joyce Dunbar

A House for Hermit Crab by Eric Carle

About Reptiles: A Guide for Children by Cathryn P. Sill

Actual Size by Steve Jenkins

Alice the Fairy by David Shannon

Alphabeasts by Wallace Edwards

Amber Waiting by Nan Gregory

Angelina's Birthday Surprise by Katharine Holabird

Are You a Snail? by Judy Allen

Be My Neighbor by Maya Ajmera

Beach Day! by Patricia Lakin

Bear Wants More by Karma Wilson

Beatrice Doesn't Want To by Laura Joffe Numeroff

Becoming Butterflies by Anne F. Rockwell

Brave, Brave Mouse by Michaela Morgan

Bubble Gum, Bubble Gum by Lisa Wheeler

Bunnies on the Go: Getting from Place to Place by Rick Walton

Can I Keep Him? by Steven Kellogg

Can You See What I See? Seymour and the Juice Box Boat by Walter Wick

Cat, What Is That? by Tony Johnston

Catalina Magdalena by Ted Arnold

Chicka Chicka 1, 2, 3 by Bill Martin

Circus Caps for Sale by Esphyr Slobodkina

Clifford the Big Red Dog books by Norman Bridwell

Cluck O'Clocky by Kes Gray

Construction Countdown by K. C. Olson

Corduroy by Don Freeman

Cowboy Bunnies by Christine Loomis

Daisy 1, 2, 3 by Peter Catalanotto

Dig Dig Digging by Margaret Mayo

Dig! by Andrea Zimmerman

Dolores on Her Toes by Barbara Samuels

Duckling by Lisa Magloff

Earthworms by Claire Llewellyn

Firefighter Frank by Monica Wellington

Five Little Monkeys Play Hide-and-Seek by Eileen Christelow

Freight Train by Donald Crews

Frog and Toad stories by Arnold Lobel

George and Martha stories by Edward Marshall

Giant Pandas by Gail Gibbons

Ginger Finds a Home by Charlotte Voake

Good Night, Harry by Kim Lewis

Goodnight, Country by Susan Verlander

Grandfather Twilight by Barbara Berger

Haircuts at Sleep Sam's by Michael R. Strickland

Hands Can by Cheryl Willis Hudson

Harold and the Purple Crayon by Crockett Johnson

Hoptoad by Jane Yolen

Hot City by Barbara M. Joosse

How Many Kisses Do You Want Tonight? by Varsha Bajaj

Hurty Feelings by Helen Lester

I Am Not Going to School Today! by Robie H. Harris

I Am Too Absolutely Small for School by Lauren Child

I Get Wet by Vicki Cobb

I Love You, Mister Bear by Sylvie Wickstrom

Jesse Bear, What Will You Wear? by Nancy Carlstrom

Keeping Quilt by Patricia Polacco

Kitten's First Full Moon by Kevin Henkes

Knuffle Bunny: A Cautionary Tale by Mo Willems

Life Cycle of a Turtle by Ron Fridell

Little Bear's Little Boat by Eve Bunting

Little Blue and Little Yellow: A Story for Pippo and Ann and Other Children
  by Leo Lionni

Little Raccoon's Big Question by Miriam Schlein

Love You Forever by Robert N. Munsch

Make Way for Ducklings by Robert McCloskey

Mary Had a Little Lamb by Mary Ann Hoberman

Max for President by Jarrett Krosoczka

Me and My Senses by Joan Sweeney

Millions of Cats by Wanda Gág

Miss Polly Has a Dolly by Pamela Duncan Edwards

Moondance by Frank Asch

Mr. George Baker by Amy Hest

Mr. Seahorse by Eric Carle

Mrs. Chicken and the Hungry Crocodile by Won-Ldy Paye

My Lucky Day by Keiko Kasza

My Teacher for President by Kay Winters

Naughty Little Monkeys by Jin Aylesworth

Oh Yeah! by Tom Birdseye

Otto Goes to Bed by Todd Parr

Peedie by Olivier Dunrea

Pie in the Sky by Lois Ehlert

Plaidypus Lost by Susan Stevens Crummel

Potty! by Mylo Freeman

Rooster Can't Cock-a-Doodle-Doo by Karen Rostoker-Gruber

Ruby in Her Own Time by Jonathan Emmett

Some Dogs Do by Jez Alborough

Some Smug Slug by Pamela Duncan Edwards

Spinning Spiders by Melvin Berger

Strega Nona by Tomie DePaola

Teeth, Tails, & Tentacles: An Animal Counting by Christopher Wormell

That's What Friends Are For by Florence Parry Heide

That's What Friends Do by Kathryn Cave

The Best Cat in the World by Leslea Newman

The Cat Who Liked Potato Soup by Terry Farish

The Day Jimmy's Boa Ate the Wash by Trinka Hakes Noble

The Day the Babies Crawled Away by Peggy Rathmann

The Hippo-NOT-amus by Tony Payne

The Kiss That Missed by David Melling

The Little Engine That Could by Watty Piper

The Little Mouse, the Red Ripe Strawberry and the Big Hungry Bear
  by Don Wood

The Neighborhood Mother Goose by Nina Crews

The Noisy Way to Bed by Ian Whybrow

The Racecar Alphabet by Brian Floca

The Runaway Bunny by Margaret Wise Brown

The Turn-Around, Upside-Down Alphabet Book by Lisa Campbell Ernst

There's a Nightmare in My Closet by Mercer Mayer

This Is the Baby by Candace Fleming

Time for Ballet by Adele Geras

Tippy-Toe Chick, Go! by George Shannon

Watch Out! by Jan Fearnley

We Use Water by Robin Nelson

What a Hat! by Holly Keller

Where Are You, Blue Kangaroo? by Emma Chichester Clark

Where Is the Green Sheep? by Mem Fox

Whistle for Willie by Ezra Jack Keats

Wild About Books by Judy Sierra

GRADES 1–2

A Fine, Fine School by Sharon Creech

A Huge Hog is a Big Pig: A Rhyming Word Game by Francis McCall

A Sip of Aesop by Jane Yolen

Albert by Donna Jo Napoli

Alien and Possum: Friends No Matter What by Tony Johnston

Almost Invisible Irene by Daphne Skinner

Alphaboat by Michael Chesworth

Amazing Bone by William Steig

Amelia Bedelia by Peggy Parish

Amelia Bedelia, Bookworm by Herman Parish

Anansi and the Magic Stick by Eric A. Kimmel

Angelina Ice Skates by Katharine Holabird

Army Ant Parade by April Pulley Sayre

Arthur and the 1,001 Dads by Stephen Krensky

Berenstein Bears stories by Stan and Jan Berenstein

Black Widow Spiders by Julie Murray

Blueberries for Sal by Robert McCloskey

Bow Wow Meow Meow: It's Rhyming Cats and Dogs by Douglas Florian

City Dog, Country Dog by Susan Stevens Crummel

Click, Clack, Moo, Cows That Type by D. Cronin

Danny and the Dinosaur Go to Camp by Syd Hoff

David books by D. Shannon

Dear Mrs. LaRue: Letters from the Investigation by Mark Teague

Dear Tooth Fairy by Jane O'Connor

Diary of a Worm by Doreen Cronin

Did Dinosaurs Have Feathers? by Kathleen Weidner Zoehfeld

Eaglet's World by Evelyn Minshull

First Flight: The Story of Tom Tate and the Wright Brothers by George Shea

First Year Letters by Julie Danneberg

Flat Stanley by Jeff Brown

Fox on the Job by James Marshall

Frog and Toad Are Friends by Arnold Lobel

Get Well, Good Knight by Shelley Moore Thomas

Goldie and the Three Bears by Diane Stanley

Goodnight Moon by Margaret Wise Brown

Gotta Go! Gotta Go! by Sam Swope

Green Eggs and Ham by Dr. Seuss

Guess How Much I Love You? by S. McBratney

Gus and Gertie and the Lucky Charms by Joan Lowery Nixon

Gus and Grandpa and the Piano Lesson by Claudia Mills

Hank Aaron: Brave in Every Way by Peter Golenbock

Hard-Times Jar by Ethel Footman Smothers

Henry and Mudge and Mrs. Hopper's House by Cynthia Rylant

High Tide in Hawaii by Mary Pope Osborne

Hooway for Wodney Wat by Helen Lester

Horses! by Gail Gibbons

If You Give a Moose a Muffin by Laura Numeroff

If You Give a Mouse a Cookie by Laura Numeroff

If You Give a Pig a Pancake by Laura Numeroff

If You Hopped Like a Frog by David Schwartz

If You Take a Mouse to the Movies by Laura Numeroff

If You're Happy and You Know It by Jan Ormerod

Incredible Sharks by Seymour Simon

Iris and Walter and Cousin Howie by Elissa Haden Guest

Is Your Mama a Llama? by Deborah Guarino

Jabuti the Tortoise: A Trickster Tale from the Amazon Rain Forest
  by Gerald McDermott

Jelly Beans for Sale by Bruce McMillan

Jesse Owens by Jane Sutcliffe

Jump, Frog, Jump by Robert Kalan

Junie B., First Grader: Toothless Wonder by Barbara Park

Kate and the Beanstalk by Mary Pope Osborne

Lionel's Birthday by Stephen Krensky

Little Bear books by Else Holmelund Minarik

Little Red Hen by Paul Galdone

Lost in the Woods: A Photographic Fantasy by Carl R. Sams and Jean Stoick

Magic Tree House series by Mary Pope Osborne

Martin's Big Words: The Life of Dr. Martin Luther King, Jr.
   by Doreen Rappaport

Marvin Redpost: A Magic Crystal? by Louis Sachar

Max and Jax in Second Grade by Jerdie Nolen

May Belle and the Ogre by Bethany Roberts

Millions of Cats by Wanda Gag

Miss Rumphius by Barbara Cooney

Mummies by Joyce Milton

My Name is Yoon by Helen Recorvits

Nate the Great on the Owl Express by Marjorie Sharmat

Nick Plays Baseball by Rachel Isadora

No Zombies Allowed by Matt Novak

Noisy Nora by Rosemary Wells

Oliver the Mighty Pig by Jean Van Leeuwen

On Noah's Ark by Jan Brett

Pinky and Rex and the Just-Right Pet by James Howe

Runaway Bunny by Margaret Wise Brown

Sam Gets Lost by Mary Labatti

Sammy the Seal by Syd Hoff

Second Grade Rules by Paula Danziger

She'll Be Comin' Around the Mountain by Philemon Sturges

Shoeless Joe and Black Betsy by Phil Bildner

Sophie Skates by Rachel Isadora

Stanley's Party by Linda Bailey

Take Me Out of the Bathtub by Alan Katz

The Cake That Mack Ate by Rose Robart

The Dog That Pitched a No-Hitter by Matt Christopher

The Doorbell Rang by Pat Hutchins

The Dot by Peter Reynolds

The Frog Prince, Continued by Jon Scieszka

The High-Rise Private Eyes: The Case of the Baffled Bear by Cynthia Rylant

The Honest-to-Goodness Truth by Patricia McKissack

The Little Mouse, the Red Ripe Strawberry and the Big Hungry Bear
  by Audrey Wood

The Little Red Ant and the Great Big Crumb by Shirley Climo

The Man Who Walked Between the Towers by Mordicai Gerstein

The Old Woman Who Lived in a Vinegar Bottle by Margaret Read MacDonald

The Pigeon Finds a Hot Dog by Mo Willems

The Seed and the Giant Saguaro by Jennifer Ward

The Trucker by Brenda Weatherby

There was a Bold Lady Who Wanted a Star by Charise Mericle Harper

Three Stories You Can Read to Your Cat by Sara Swan Miller

Trouble on the T-Ball Team by Eve Bunting

Wait! No Paint! by Bruce Whatley

What About Me? by Ed Young

What Do You Do With a Tail Like This? by Steve Jenkins

Why Do Birds Sing? by Joan Holub

You Read to Me, I'll Read to You: Very Short Fairy Tales to Read Together
  by Mary Ann Hoberman

Young Cam Jansen and the Double Beach Mystery by David Adler

Yummy Riddles by Marilyn Helmer

Zelda and Ivy the Boy Next Door by Laura McGee Kvasnosky

GRADES 3–4

"Secrets of Droon" series by Tony Abbott

A Picture Book of Lewis and Clark by David A. Adler

Alice in Wonderland and *Through the Looking Glass* by Lewis Carroll

Animal Ark books by Baglio

Anne of Green Gables by L. M. Montgomery

BFG by Roald Dahl

Birthday Pony by Jessie Haas

Black Stallion by Walter Farley

Boxcar Children series by Gertrude Chandler Warner

Charlie and the Chocolate Factory by Roald Dahl

Charlotte's Web by E. B. White

Children of the Dragon: Selected Tales from Vietnam by Sherry Garland

Children of the Lamp by P. Kerr

Danny Champion of the World by Roald Dahl

Davey's Blue Eyed Frog by Patricia Harrison Easton

Dog Days by David Lubar

Dogs by Seymour Simon

Dogsong by Gary Paulsen

Double Fudge by Judy Blume

Encyclopedia Brown, Boy Detective by Donald Sobol

Falling Up by Shel Silverstein

Fourth Grade Fuss by Johanna Hurwitz

Freddy In Peril: Book Two In the Golden Hamster Saga by Dietlof Reiche

Fudge-a-mania by Judy Blume

Girl Wonder: A Baseball Story in Nine Innings by Deborah Hopkinson

Good Grief Third Grade by Colleen O'Shaughnessy McKenna

Gooney Bird Greene by Lois Lowry

Growing Up Wild: Wolves by Sandra Markle

Hachiko: The True Story of a Loyal Dog by Pamela S. Turner

Hatchet by Gary Paulsen

Heidi by Johanna Spyri

Help! Somebody Get Me Out of Fourth Grade by Hank Zipzer

High as a Hawk: A Brave Girl's Historic Climb by T. A. Barron

Holes by Louis Sachar

How to Train Your Dragon by Cressida Cowell

Hurricanes by Seymour Simon

If the World Were a Village by David J. Smith

It Came from Beneath the Bed! by James Howe

Jake Drake, Class Clown by Andrew Clements

James and the Giant Peach by Roald Dahl

Judy Moody by Megan McDonald

Judy Moody Predicts the Future by Megan McDonald

Lighthouse Family: The Eagle by Cynthia Rylant

Lily's Crossing by Patricia Reilly Giff

Little House in the Big Woods by Laura Ingalls Wilder

Loser by Jerry Spinelli

Magic Tree House series by Mary Pope Osborne

Mallory on the Move by Laurie Friedman and Tamara Schmitz

Maniac Magee by Jerry Spinelli

Mary Margaret and the Perfect Pet Plan by Christine MacLean

Mathematickles by Betsy Franco

Matilda by Roald Dahl

Me Oh Maya by Jon Scieszka

Meow Means Mischief by Ann Whitehead Nagda

Mightier Than the Sword: World Folktales for Strong Boys by Jane Yolen

Mister and Me by Kimberly Willis Holt

Mr. Popper's Penguins by Richard Atwater

Ms. Frizzle's Adventures: Medieval Castle by Joanna Cole

Muggie Maggie by Beverly Cleary

Mummies, Pyramids, and Pharaohs: A Book About Ancient Egypt by Gail Gibbons

My Brother, Martin: A Sister Remembers Growing Up with The Rev. Dr. Martin Luther King, Jr. by Christine Farris

My Dog, My Hero by Betsy Byers

My Rotten Red-Headed Older Brother by Patricia Polacco

No Dogs Allowed by Bill Wallace

Noah's Ark by Jerry Pinkney

Odd Boy Out: Young Albert Einstein by Don Brown

Otherwise Known as Sheila the Great by Judy Blume

Outside and Inside Giant Squids by Sandra Markle

Owen Foote, Mighty Scientist by Stephanie Greene

Perfectly Chelsea by Claudia Mills

Pigs Can Fly!: The Adventures of Harriet Pig and Friends by Debbi Chocolate

Pocahontas; Lewis and Clark by George Sullivan

Rainbow Soup by Brian P. Cleary

Ramona Quimby by Beverly Cleary

Ramona's World by Beverly Cleary

Rickie and Henri: A True Story by Jane Goodall

Runaway Ralph by Beverly Cleary

Sacagawea by Lise Erdrich

Scranimals by Jack Prelutsky

Secret Garden by Frances Hodgson Burnett

Secret Identity: Shredderman by Wendelin Van Draanen

Shiloh by Phyllis Reynolds Naylor

Sideways Stories by Louis Sachar

Sign of the Beaver by Elizabeth George Speare

Sleeping Beauty by Mahlon F. Craft

So You Want to Be an Inventor? by Judith St. George

Stone Fox by John R. Gardiner

Stuart Little by E. B. White

Superfudge by Judy Blume

Tales of a Fourth Grade Nothing by Judy Blume

The 5,000-Year-Old Puzzle by Claudia Logan

The Boxcar Children books by Gertrude Chandler Warner

The Boy on Fairfield Street: How Ted Geisel Grew Up to Become Dr. Seuss
  by Kathleen Krull

The Boy Who Spoke Dog by Clay Morgan

The Castle in the Attic by Elizabeth Winthrop

The Cat Who Got Away by Allan Ahlberg

The Countess's Calamity by Sally Gardner

*The End of the Beginning: Being the Adventures of a Small Snail (and an Even
  Smaller Ant)* by Avi

The Fish in Room 11 by Heather Dyer

The Girl Who Spun Gold by Virginia Hamilton

The Giving Tree by Shel Silverstein

The Great Serum Race: Blazing the Iditarod Trail by Debbie S. Miller

The Lady and the Lion by Laurel Long and Jacqueline K. Ogburn

The Legend of Spud Murphy by Eoin Colfer

The Mayor of Central Park by Avi

The Mouse and the Motorcycle by Beverly Cleary

The Mummy's Mother by Tony Johnson

The Nine Lives of Aristotle by Dick King-Smith

The Report Card by Andrew Clements

The Secret Knowledge of Grown-ups: The Second File by David Wisniewski

The Story of a Seagull and the Cat Who Taught Her to Fly by Luis Sepulveda

The Weeping Willow: An Ike and Mem Story by Patrick Jennings

The World According to Humphrey by Betty Birney

There's a Frog in My Throat: 440 Animal Sayings a Little Bird Told Me
  by Loreen Leedy and Pat Street

Toad Rage by Morris Gleitzman

Treasury of Elves and Fairies by Jane Werner Watson

Trumpet of the Swan by E. B. White

Unwitting Wisdom: An Anthology of Aesop's Fables by Helen Ward

Utterly Me, Clarice Bean by Lauren Child

Whales! Strange and Wonderful by Laurence Pringle

Where the Red Fern Grows by Wilson Rawls

White Star: A Dog on the Titanic by Marty Crisp

Wildfire by Elizabeth Starr Hill

Wonderful Story of Henry Sugar by Roald Dahl

Wonderful Words: Poems About Reading, Writing, Speaking and Listening
  by Lee Bennett Hopkins

GRADES 5–6

A Face First by Priscilla Cummings

A Long Way from Chicago by Richard Peck

A Ring of Endless Light by Madeleine L'Engle

A Week in the Woods by Andrew Clements

A Young Patriot: The American Revolution as Experienced by One Boy
  by Jim Murphy

Al Capone Does My Shirts by Gennifer Choldenko

Amelia's War by Ann Rinaldi

America's Great Disasters by Martin W. Sandler

Among the Hidden by Margaret Peterson Haddix

Artemis Fowl by Eoin Colfer

Becoming Naomi Leon by Pam Muñoz Ryan

Bird by Angela Johnson

Bound by Donna Jo Napoli

Bridge to Terabithia by Katherine Paterson

Bud, Not Buddy by Christopher Paul Christopher

Buttermilk Hill by Ruth White

Carver: A Life in Poems by Marilyn Nelson

Charlie's Raven by Jean Craighead George

Chasing Vermeer by Blue Balliett

Chu Ju's House by Gloria Whelan

Crispin: The Cross of Lead by Avi

Dealing with Dragons by Patricia Wrede

Digging for Bird-dinosaurs: An Expedition to Madagascar by Nic Bishop

Ella Enchanted by Gail Carson Levine

Eragon by Christopher Paolini

Escape from Saigon: How a Vietnam War Orphan Became an American Boy
  by Andrea Warren

Eureka! : Poems About Inventors by Joyce Sidman

Fair Weather by Richard Peck

Fever, 1793 by Laurie Halse Anderson

Fish by L. S. Matthews

Frindle by Andrew Clements

George Washington, Spymaster: How the Americans Outspied the British and
  Won the Revolutionary War by Thomas B. Allen

Gregor the Overlander by Suzanne Collins

Hatchet by Gary Paulsen

Heart to Heart: New Poems Inspired by Twentieth-Century Art
  by Jan Greenberg, ed.

Heartbeat by Sharon Creech

Hero Dogs: Courageous Canines in Action by Donna M. Jackson

Hoot by Carl Hiaasen

How I Found the Strong: A Civil War Story by Margaret McMullen

*Ida B: ...And Her Plans to Maximize Fun, Avoid Disaster, and (Possibly) Save
  the World* by Katherine Hannigan

In the Days of the Vaqueros: America's First True Cowboys
  by Russell Freedman

Inkheart by Cornelia Caroline Funke

Iqbal: A Novel by Francesco D'Adamo

Is This Forever or What?: Poems and Paintings from Texas
  by Naomi Shihab Nye

Island of the Aunts by Eva Ibbotson

Jason's Gold by Will Hobbs

Jip: His Story by Katherine Patterson

Joey Pigza Swallowed the Key by Jack Gantos

Journey to the River Sea by Eva Ibbotson

Julie's Wolf Pack by Jean Craighead George

Just Ella by Margaret Peterson Haddix

Killer Rocks from Outer Space: Asteroids, Comets, and Meteorites
  by Steven N. Koppes

King of Shadows by Susan Cooper

Kira-kira by Cynthia Kadohata

Langston Hughes, American Poet by Alice Walker

Letters from Camp by Kate Klise

Little Women by Louisa May Alcott

Macaroni Boy by Katherine Ayres

Maggie's Door by Patricia Reilly Giff

Mickey and Me: A Baseball Card Adventure by Dan Gutman

Mrs. Frisby and the Rats of Nimh by Robert C. O'Brien

My Louisiana Sky by Kimberly Willis Holt

Nancy Drew books by Carolyn Keene

Never Mind!: A Twin Novel by Avi

North by Donna Jo Napoli

Number the Stars by Lois Lowry

Olive's Ocean by Kevin Henkes

One Unhappy Horse by C. S. Adler

Painters of the Caves by Patricia Lauber

Peter and the Starcatchers by Dave Barry

Regarding the Fountain by Kate Klise

Rodzina by Karen Cushman

Rowan Hood, Outlaw Girl of Sherwood by Nancy Springer

Saffy's Angel by Hilary McKay

Sahara Special by Esme Raji Codell

Saving Shiloh by Phyllis Reynolds Naylor

Second Cousins by Virginia Hamilton

Seven Wonders of the Ancient World by Lynn Curlee

Shades of Gray by Carolyn Reeder

Shatterglass by Tamora Pierce

Star in the Storm by Joan Hiatt Harlow

Sticks by Joan Bauer

Swear to Howdy by Wendelin Van Draanen

Ten Kings: And the Worlds They Ruled by Milton Meltzer

The Boy Who Saved Baseball by John Ritter

The Captain's Dog by Roland Smith

The Chronicles of Narnia books by C. S. Lewis

The Devil's Arithmetic by Jane Yolen

The Edge Chronicles by P. Stewart

The Future Is Wild by Dougal Dixon

The Gawgon and the Boy by Lloyd Alexander

The Goose Girl by Shannon Hale

The Graduation of Jake Moon by Barbara Park

The Great Good Thing by Roderick Townley

The Greatest: Muhammad Ali by Walter Dean Myers

The Green Dog: A Mostly True Story by Suzanne Fisher Staples

The Hardy Boys books by Franklin W. Dixon

The Janitor's Boy by Andrew Clements

The Kidnappers: A Mystery by Willo Davis Roberts

The Landry News by Andrew Clements

The Lost Years of Merlin by T. A. Barron

The Man Who Made Time Travel by Kathryn Lasky

The Music of Dolphins by Karen Hesse

The Mystery of the Black Moriah by David A. Crossman

The Old Willis Place: A Ghost Story by Mary Dowling Hahn

The Outcasts of 19 Schuyler Place by E. L. Konigsberg

The Pepins and Their Problems by Polly Horvath

The Pirates of Pompeii by Caroline Lawrence

The School Story by Andrew Clements

The Sea of Trolls by Nancy Farmer

The Seeing Stone by Kevin Crossley-Holland

The Tale of Despereaux: Being the Story of a Mouse, a Princess, Some Soup, and a Spool of Thread by Kate DiCamillo

The Tarantula Scientist by Sy Montgomery

The Teacher's Funeral: A Comedy in Three Parts by Richard Peck

The Unseen by Zilpha Keatley Snyder

The View from Saturday by E. L. Konigsberg

The Watsons Go to Birmingham by Christopher Paul Curtis

Through My Eyes by Ruby Bridges

Troubling a Star by Madeleine L'Engle

Tuck Everlasting by Natalie Babbitt

Walt Whitman: Words for America by Barbara Kerley

William Shakespeare's Hamlet by Bruce Coville

With Cloth and Courage: Winning the Fight for a Woman's Right to Vote by Ann Bausum

World Afire by Paul B. Janeczko

GRADES 7–8

20,000 Leagues Under the Sea by Jules Verne

A Corner of the Universe by Ann M. Martin

A Matter of Profit by Hilari Bell

A Pocket Full of Rye by Agatha Christie

A Prayer for Owen Meany: A Novel by John Irving

Abhorsen by Garth Nix

After the Death of Anna Gonzalez by Terri Fields

Airborne by Kenneth Oppel

All-American Girl by Meg Cabot

Amulet of Samarkand by Jonathan Stroud

An American Hero: The True Story of Charles A. Lindbergh
  by Barry Denenberg

An American Plague: The True and Terrifying Story of the Yellow Fever
  Epidemic of 1793 by Jim Murphy

Andromeda Strain by Michael Crichton

B for Buster by Iain Lawrence

Babe Didrickson Zaharias by Russell Freedman

Before We Were Free by Julia Alvarez

Black Diamond: The Story of the Negro Baseball Leagues
  by Patricia McKissack

Black Potatoes by Susan Campbell Bartoletti

Boy at War: A Novel of Pearl Harbor by Harry Mazer

Brady by Jean Fritz

Brave New World by Aldous Huxley

Bridge to Terabithia by Katherine Paterson

California Blue by D. Klass

Castle in the Air by Diana Wynne Jones

City of the Beasts by Isabel Allende

Cold Mountain by Charles Frazier

Cold Sassy Tree by Olive Ann Burns

Colibr by Ann Cameron

Crash by Jerry Spinelli

Crazy Lady by J. Conly

Danger Zone by David Klass

Daughter of Venice by Donna Jo Napoli

Deathwatch by Robb White

Dracula by Bram Stoker

Dust to Eat: Drought and Depression in the 1930s by Michael Cooper

Eager by Helen Fox

Earthquake at Dawn by Kristina Gregory

Ender's Game by Orson Scott Card

Eragon by Christopher Paolini

Fantastic Voyage by Isaac Asimov

Fire Bringer by David Clement-Davies

Flags of Our Fathers: Heroes of Iwo Jima by James Bradley;
  adapted by Michael French

Gathering of Old Men by Ernest J. Gaines

Halfway to the Sky by Kimberly Brubaker Bradley

Heir Apparent by Vivian Vande Velde

High Heat by Carl Deuker

Homeless Bird by Gloria Whelan

Hoops by Walter Dean

House of the Scorpion by Nancy Farmer

Howl's Moving Castle by Diana Wynne Jones

Hush by Jacqueline Woodson

I Know What You Did Last Summer by Lois Duncan

Into the Wild by Jon Krakauer

Izzy, Willy-Nilly by Cynthia Voight

Jane Eyre by Charlotte Bronte

Jason's Gold by Will Hobbs

Keeper of the Night by Kimberly Willis Holt

Left for Dead. A Young Man's Search for Justice for the USS Indianapolis
  by Peter Nelson

Let It Shine: Stories of Black Women Freedom Fighters
  by Andrea Davis Pinkney

Lincoln: A Photobiography by Russell Freedman

Make Lemonade by Virginia Euwer Wolff

Maniac Magee by Jerry Spinelli

Milkweed by Jerry Spinelli

Monster by Walter Dean Meyers

Montmorency, Thief, Liar, Gentleman? by Eleanor Updale

Moves Make the Man by Bruce Brooks

Never Cry Wolf by Farley Mowat

Nine Days a Queen by Ann Rinaldi

Nothing but the Truth by Avi

Olive's Ocean by Kevin Henkes

Parvana's Journey by Deborah Ellis

Phoenix Rising by Karen Hesse

Police Lab: How Forensic Science Tracks Down and Convicts Criminals
   by David Owen

Rumble Fish by S. E. Hinton

Running Out of Time by Margaret P. Haddix

Sang Spell by Phyllis Reynolds Naylor

Secrets in the House of Delgado by Gloria Miklowitz

Shadow Spinner by Susan Fletcher

Shakespeare Bats Clean Up by Ron Koertge

Ship of Fire by Michael Cadnum

Shipwreck at the Bottom of the World by Jennifer Armstrong

Sign of the Four by Sir Arthur Conan Doyle

Silent to the Bone by E. L. Konigsburg

Six Days in October: The Stock Market Crash of 1929 by Karen Blumenthal

Soldier Boys by Dean Hughes

Sorceress by Celia Rees

Sparrow Hawk Red by Ben Mikaelsen

Spindle's End by Robin McKinley

Stand Tall by Joan Bauer

Stargirl by Jerry Spinelli

Stones in Water by Donna Jo Napoli

Stowaway by Karen Hesse

Stravaganza: City of Masks by Mary Hoffman

Stuck in Neutral by Terry Trueman

Supernaturalist by Eoin Colfer

Surviving Hitler: A Boy in the Nazi Death Camps by Andrea Warren

Tangerine by Edward Bloor

Tell Them We Remember: The Story of the Holocaust by Susan Bachrach

The Adventures of Tom Sawyer by Mark Twain

The Amber Spyglass by Phillip Pullman

The Call of the Wild by Jack London

The Chocolate War by Robert Cormier

The Girls by Amy Goldman Koss

The Grape Thief by Kristine L. Franklin

The Grapes of Wrath by John Steinbeck

The Hideout by Eve Bunting

The Hobbit, or There and Back Again by J. R. R. Tolkien

The Hunting of the Last Dragon by Sherryl Jordan

The Killer Angels by Michael Shaara

The Land by Mildred Taylor

The Last Silk Dress by Ann Rinaldi

The Midwife's Apprentice by Karen Cushman

The Misfits by James Howe

The Mississippi Trial, 1955 by Chris Crowe

The Mozart Season by Virginia E. Wolff

The Music of Dolphins by Karen Hesse

The Other Side of Truth by Beverley Naidoo

The Outsiders by S. E. Hinton

The Pigman by Paul Zindel

The Princess Diaries by Meg Cabot

The Ramsey Scallop by Frances Temple

The Rifle by Gary Paulsen

The River Between Us by Richard Peck

The Ropemaker by Peter Dickinson

The Sally Lockheart Trilogy: The Ruby in the Smoke, The Shadow in the North,
  The Tiger in the Well by Phillip Pullman

The Secret Life of Bees by Sue Monk Kidd

The Secret of Sarah Revere by Ann Rinaldi

The Shakespeare Stealer by Gary Blackwood

The Slave Dancer by Paula Fox

The Subtle Knife (His Dark Materials Book 2) by Phillip Pullman

The Tale of Despereaux by Kate DiCamillo

The Thief Lord by Cornelia Funke

The Time Machine by H. G. Wells

The True Confessions of Charlotte Doyle by Avi

The Westing Game by Ellen Raskin

The Wizard of Earthsea by Ursula LeGuin

The Wreckers by Iain Lawrence

The Young Man and the Sea by Rodman Philbrick

Their Eyes Were Watching God by Zora Neale Hurston

Thura's Diary: My Life in Wartime Iraq by Thura Al-Windawi

Ties That Bind, Ties That Break by Lensey Namioka

Tomorrowland: 10 Stories About the Future by Michael Cart (compiler)

Trembling Earth by Kim L. Siegelson

Trickster's Choice by Tamora Pierce

Triss by Brian Jacques

Trouble With Lemons by Daniel Hayes

Tuesdays with Morrie by Mitch Albom

Tunes for Bears to Dance to by Robert Cormier

Wee Free Men by Terry Pratchett

When My Name Was Keoko by Linda Sue Park

Whirligig by Paul Fleischman

White Lilacs by Carolyn Meyer

Why Do Buses Come in Threes? The Hidden Mathematics in Everyday Life
  by Robert Eastaway

Wild Man Island by Will Hobbs

Within Reach: My Everest Story by Mark Pfetzer

Witness by Karen Hesse

Wolf by the Ears by Ann Rinaldi

Wringer by Jerry Spinelli

Zel by Donna Jo Napoli

Zlata's Diary: A Child's Life in Sarajevo by Zlata Filipovic

GRADES 9–10

19 Varieties of Gazelle: Poems of the Middle East by Naomi Shihab Nye

A Farewell to Arms by Ernest Hemingway

Abraham: A Journey to the Heart of Three Faiths by Bruce Feiler

All Over but the Shoutin' by Rick Bragg

Blessings: A Novel by Anna Quindlen

Catcher in the Rye by J. D. Salinger

Chinese Cinderella by Adeline Yen Mah

Crazy Loco: Stories by David Rice

Crow Lake: A Novel by Mary Lawson

Damage by A. M. Jenkins

Dune by Frank Herbert

Ender's Shadow by Orson Scott Card

Evidence of Things Unseen: A Novel by Marianne Wiggins

Eye of the World by Robert Jordan

Fallen Angels by Walter Dean Myers

Finding Their Stride by Sally Pont

Friday Night Lights: A Town, a Team, and a Dream by H. G. Bissinger

Girl with a Pearl Earring by Tracy Chevalier

Going Postal by Terry Pratchett

Gone With the Wind by Margaret Mitchell

Hitchhiker's Guide to the Galaxy by Douglas Adams

Hole in My Life by Jack Gantos

It's Not About the Bike: My Journey Back to Life by Lance Armstrong

Jane Eyre by Charlotte Brontë

Kaffir Boy: The True Story of a Black Youth's Coming of Age in Apartheid South Africa by Mark Mathabane

Light-Gathering Poems by Liz Rosenberg

Maisie Dobbs by Jacqueline Winspear

Mr. Midshipman Hornblower by C. S. Forester

My Losing Season by Pat Conroy

Native Son by Richard Wright

Nectar in a Sieve by Kamala Markandaya

Neverwhere by Neil Giaman

Paper Mage by Leah R. Cutter

Peace Like a River by Leif Enger

Persepolis: the Story of a Childhood by Marjane Satrapi

Rebecca by Daphne du Maurier

Seabiscuit: An American Legend by Laura Hillenbrand

Selected Poems: Carl Sandburg by Carl Sandburg

Shadow Divers: The True Adventure of Two Americans Who Risked Everything to Solve One of the Last Mysteries of World War II by Robert Kurson

Silent Night: The Remarkable 1914 Christmas Truce by Stanley Weintraub

Slaughterhouse Five by Kurt Vonnegut

Son of the Mob by Gordon Korman

Speak by Laurie Halse Anderson

Stiff: The Curious Lives of Human Cadavers by Mary Roach

The Blue Lawn by William Taylor

The Curious Incident of the Dog in the Nighttime by Mark Haddon

The Golden Compass by Philip Pullman

The House of the Seven Gables by Nathaniel Hawthorne

The Life of Pi: A Novel by Yann Martel

The No. 1 Ladies' Detective Agency by Alexander McCall Smith

The Once and Future King by T. H. White

The School of Beauty and Charm by Melanie Sumner

The Secret Life of Bees by Sue Monk Kidd

The Sisterhood of the Traveling Pants by Ann Brashears

Truth and Bright Water by Thomas King

Versos Sencillos/Simple Verses by José Marti

Voices from Vietnam by Barry Denenberg

We Are All the Same: A Story of a Boy's Courage and a Mother's Love by Jim Wooten

West of Kabul, East of New York: An Afghan American Story by Tamin Ansary

Whale Talk by Chris Crutcher

Women of the Silk by Gail Tsukiyama

Year of Wonders: A Novel of the Plague by Geraldine Brooks

You Don't Know Me: A Novel by David Klass

GRADES 11–12

A Brief History of Time: From the Big Bang to Black Holes
  by Stephen Hawking

A Chorus for Peace: A Global Anthology of Poetry by Women
  by Marilyn Arnold, Bonnie Ballif-Spanville and Kristen Tracy, editors

A Death in Texas: A Story of Race, Murder and a Small Town's Struggle for
  Redemption by Dina Temple-Raston

All Loves Excelling: A Novel by Josiah Bunting

Almost a Woman by Esmeralda Santiago

America: A Novel by E. R. Frank

And Still We Rise: The Trials and Triumphs of Twelve Gifted Inner-City
  Students by Miles Corwin

Atonement: A Novel by Ian McEwan

Balzac and the Little Chinese Seamstress by Dai Siije

Bonesetter's Daughter by Amy Tan

Born Confused by Tanuja Desai Hidier

Breathing Underwater by Alexandra Flinn

Catch-22 by Joseph Heller

Chronicle of a Death Foretold by Gabriel Garcia Marquez

Crime and Punishment by Fyodor Dostoyevsky

Devil in the White City: Murder, Magic, and Madness at the Fair That Changed
  America by Erik Larson

Don't Let's Go to the Dogs Tonight: An African Childhood by Alexandra Fuller

Drinking Coffee Elsewhere by Z. Z. Packer

Ella Minnow Pea: A Novel in Letters by Mark Dunn

Fast Food Nation: The Dark Side of the All-American Meal by Eric Schlosser

Founding Mothers: the Women Who Raised Our Nation by Cokie Roberts

Go Tell It On the Mountain by James Baldwin

Hamlet's Dresser: A Memoir by Bob Smith

How the Cows Turned Mad by Maxime Schwartz

In Code: A Mathematical Journey by Sarah Flannery with David Flannery

In Cold Blood: A True Account of a Multiple Murder and Its Consequences
  by Truman Capote

Invisible Man by Ralph Ellison

Lonesome Dove by Larry McMurtry

Middlesex by Jeffrey Eugenidies

Nickel and Dimed: On (Not) Getting By in America by Barbara Ehrenreich

On Writing: A Memoir of the Craft by Stephen King

One Writer's Beginnings by Eudora Welty

Oryx and Crake: A Novel by Margaret Atwood

Palace Walk by Naguib Mahfouz

Pride and Prejudice by Jane Austen

Sailing Alone Around the Room by Billy Collins

Scourge: The Once and Future Threat of Smallpox by Jonathan B. Tucker

Six Easy Pieces by Richard Feynman

Stranger in a Strange Land by Robert Heinlein

Tell No One by Harlan Coben

The Autobiography of Malcolm X by Alex Haley

The Bell Jar by Sylvia Plath

The Bluest Eye by Toni Morrison

The Bookseller of Kabul by Asne Seierstad

The Color of Water by James McBride

The Future of Life by Edward O. Wilson

The Grapes of Wrath by John Steinbeck

The Kite Runner by Khaled Hosseini

The Known World by Edward P. Jones

The Lady and the Unicorn by Tracy Chevalier

The Lords of Discipline by Pat Conroy

The Modern American Presidency by Lewis Gould

The Namesake by Jhumpa Lahiri

The Plot Against America by Philip Roth

The Time Traveler's Wife by Audrey Niffenegger

The Tipping Point: How Little Things Can Make a Big Difference
  by Malcolm Gladwell

Twenty Love Poems and a Song of Despair by Pablo Neruda

Under the Banner of Heaven: A Story of Violent Faith by Jon Krakauer

Waiting: A Novel by Jin Ha

Walden by Henry David Thoreau

We Band of Angels: The Untold Story of American Nurses Trapped on Bataan by the Japanese by Elizabeth Norman

West with the Night by Beryl Markham

Will in the World: How Shakespeare Became Shakespeare by Stephen Greenblatt

Woman Hollering Creek and Other Stories by Sandra Cisneros

SUGGESTED INTERNET RESOURCES

www.reading.org
www.cbcbooks.org
www.ala.org/alsc

INDEX